# MINIMALISM AND TIME MANAGEMENT

2-in-1 Book

Simple Yet Effective Strategies to Declutter Your Mind and Increase Your Productivity by Learning Minimalist Smart Habits (Beginner's Guide)

# MINIMALISM & DECLUTTERING: GOODBYE THINGS, HELLO FREEDOM

*Discover Cutting Edge Methods to Declutter Your Mind and Live A More Fulfilled Life with Less (Beginner's Guide)*

© Copyright 2019 - All rights reserved.

The following book is reproduced below with the goal of providing information that is as accurate and reliable as possible. Regardless, purchasing this book can be seen as consent to the fact that both the publisher and the author of this book are in no way experts on the topics discussed within and that any recommendations or suggestions that are made herein are for entertainment purposes only. Professionals should be consulted as needed prior to undertaking any of the action endorsed herein.

This declaration is deemed fair and valid by both the American Bar Association and the Committee of Publishers Association and is legally binding throughout the United States.

Furthermore, the transmission, duplication, or reproduction of any of the following work including specific information will be considered an illegal act irrespective of if it is done electronically or in print. This extends to creating a secondary or tertiary copy of the work or a recorded copy and is only allowed with the express written consent from the Publisher. All additional rights reserved.

The information in the following pages is broadly considered a truthful and accurate account of facts and as such, any inattention, use, or misuse of the information in question by the reader will render any resulting actions solely under their purview. There are no scenarios in which the publisher or the original author of this work can be in any fashion deemed liable for any hardship or damages that may befall them after undertaking information described herein.

Additionally, the information in the following pages is intended only for informational purposes and should thus be thought of as universal. As befitting its nature, it is presented without assurance regarding its prolonged validity or interim quality. Trademarks that are mentioned are done without written consent and can in no way be considered an endorsement from the trademark holder.

Minimalism & Decluttering

# Table of Contents

INTRODUCTION .................................................................................. 7

## CHAPTER ONE - UNDERSTANDING MINIMALISM ....................... 10
What is Minimalism? ......................................................................... 10
Minimalism vs. the Culture of Consumerism .......................................... 11
8 Life-Altering Benefits of Minimalism .................................................. 12
The Relationship between Minimalism and Decluttering ....................... 14
The Warning Signs Signaling Clutter that You Cannot Ignore ................. 15

## CHAPTER TWO - LAYING THE FOUNDATION FOR YOUR BEST MINIMALIST SELF .............................................................................. 18
Powerful Principles to Help You See the World as a True Minimalist .... 18
Everyday Minimalist Habits to Get You In the Zone ............................. 25

## CHAPTER THREE - DECLUTTER YOUR HOME 101 ........................ 32
Light Decluttering: How do I start? ..................................................... 32
Tips to Maintain a Permanently Decluttered Home .............................. 33
Questions You Must Ask Yourself Before You Buy Anything ................. 43
The 30-Day Wishlist Strategy ............................................................. 44

## CHAPTER FOUR - FREE YOURSELF FROM EMOTIONAL AND MENTAL CLUTTER ............................................................................ 46
Factors that Facilitate Mental Clutter .................................................. 47
Must-Know Practices to Help You Deal with Mental Clutter ................. 48
How to Identify Your Core Values ....................................................... 54
Everything You Need to Know About Decluttering Your Relationships . 55

## CHAPTER FIVE – THE SECRETS OF FINANCIAL MINIMALISM ......... 65
How Minimalism Can Help You Financially ........................................... 65
Minimalist Tips to Help You Achieve Financial Freedom ....................... 66

## CHAPTER SIX - ADVANCED HOME DECLUTTERING ...................... 71
A Room-by-Room Decluttering Guide ................................................. 71
Tips for Getting Rid of Sentimental Clutter ......................................... 74

The Best Way to Decorate and Design a Minimalist Home ............... 75

## CHAPTER SEVEN - DIGITAL DECLUTTERING ................... 77
The Principles of Digital Minimalism ...................... 78
Important Advice for Defeating Digital Clutter ....................... 78

## CHAPTER EIGHT - PERFECTING THE MINIMALISM EXPERIENCE .... 82
Why We Need Experiences More Than Material Things ...................... 82
Experiences that are Better Than Any Material Object You Can Buy ..... 84
The Experiences that Make Far Better Gifts than 'Stuff' ...................... 86

## CONCLUSION ................................................................. 90

Minimalism & Decluttering

# INTRODUCTION

It can happen in the blink of an eye: one day you wake up and discover your life is clogged. You realize you don't really need most of the stuff you currently own. You discover you have slipped into the black hole of clutter and if care is not taken, you could slip even deeper and lose the true essence of your life. The possessions around your home could fall into any of these categories: things bought, things Inherited, and gifts received. At one point or another in your life, all these things served a particular purpose. You were happy with them, until you realized you no longer needed them. These items were tossed into a space of your home and began to occupy it permanently. Over time, stuff has accumulated and now you've lost control. It's like you are a protagonist in a horror movie and all these items have invaded your home with the sole aim of tormenting you.

You have picked up the right book. I can assure you of that. In these chapters, I will be exposing less-known ways of reclaiming your life, your mind, and your finances. It is one thing to notice the presence of clutter in your life, but it is another thing to know how to get rid of it. People tend to ignore the clutter in their lives, not because they are comfortable with it, but because they don't know how to relieve themselves of it. This can be the most frustrating of all. In fact, it is better not to discover the presence of clutter than to discover it and not know what to do about it. Truth is, clutter can easily become so large and towering that you can't help but notice it. These monsters of clutter are why I embarked on this journey. With my wealth of knowledge in your arsenal, you'll defeat clutter in no time.

I like to refer to myself as a "Declutter Agent." It may sound strange (you may be wondering, "Is that really a thing? Do people study that at school?") but we exist, believe me. People in modern day are finally willing to let go of the junk hoarded in their basements and attics, and experts like me help them achieve this aim. From the young age of seven, I began what I fondly call "An Experiment on Clutter." It is a work in progress, but I have discovered valuable information on how to starve clutter of their life force and hinder their growth. There is an antidote to this monster's bite!

The antidote is this: minimalism and decluttering. The two go hand-in-hand and the wonders they work in your home and life are startlingly transformative.

In the ignorant mind, the word 'minimalism' can sometimes conjure visions of poverty, extreme frugality or even stinginess. This view is completely inaccurate. Minimalism puts you in control of your life. Know how they say, "less is more"? Minimalism and its approach to decluttering will help you reclaim all personal spaces that have been eaten up by junk. Your home will finally become a place where you can live freely, unobstructed, and life will become more enjoyable and fulfilling, overall. It is possible to achieve this!

The study of minimalism and decluttering is one that I have dedicated a great deal of my life and career to. And many of my past clients rave about the positive results they've seen after employing the methods taught in my seminars and webinars. Many of my clients have overcome depression and anxiety, and the majority have learned to regain control over their chaotic lives. These glowing testimonials have compelled me to compile an up-to-date and highly comprehensive archive of my methods. These are the same tools and techniques I teach to my clients. People who adhere to my instructions rarely find themselves coming face-to-face with clutter again. All you need is the right dose of self-discipline and you are good to go.

The approach I bring to the topic of decluttering and minimalism is a simple and straightforward one. I understand that some of my readers will be first-time students of the topic, so it'll be best if it is watered down for their easy understanding. The act of decluttering can be mistaken as a sequence of actions that involve the process organizing or putting things in their right places, but I tell you there is more to it than that. The ultimate success of the process is dependent on mindset and a determination to maintain consistency. I will not only teach you how to declutter your home, I will also show you how to declutter your life, your mind and your thoughts. It is an all round process, and if one facet is ignored, then success might never be attained.

Think of the clutter in your life as an ever increasing monster. There is no stopping its growth. As time goes on, you will acquire more household items, kitchen utensils, children toys and clothes. All these things will accumulate and pile into corners of the home. All of these might not appear dangerous in the real sense of danger, but clutter is a life poison, a virus that slows down the operating system of your life. Understand that your home, mind, business and family are all at stake because of the presence of clutter.

A Chinese proverb says that the best time to plant a tree is twenty years ago. The second best time is now. The solution isn't only in taking action, but in taking the necessary action NOW! No matter how stirred you may be by the points detailed in this book, you will never achieve tangible minimalism success until you begin to apply the methods listed. You'll feel a push while reading this book; don't hold back. Draw out a small timetable for yourself and stick to it. Make a conscious effort to declutter your life. Remember, only you can help you out.

# CHAPTER ONE - UNDERSTANDING MINIMALISM

## What is Minimalism?

The term 'minimalism' originated from an extreme form of abstract art that was first developed in the U.S in the early 1960s. This form of art depicted imagery that was stripped down to its barest so it could be more easily understood while passing across the intended message. The qualities of minimalist art were that they held a form of purified beauty for any beholder willing to look past their stripped down nature. In essence, the basic message that minimalist artists wanted to send was that there is always more in less. And as counter-intuitive as that sounded, the art form excelled and became popular with time. To help you understand its popularity, Alberto Giacometti's simple human-scale bronze sculpture of a pointing man sold for a whopping $141.3 million in May 2015.

The truth is that the concept of minimalism has been popular for centuries, even though many people have mistakenly assumed it to be a modern phenomenon. Minimalism has always been linked to pure, intentional art and design concepts. But it is also much more than that. Minimalism is about identifying the basics, the necessities, and sticking with them while eliminating all excess.

Our lives in this modern world are far from minimalist. Our society is constantly fed with the notion that the more you have, the more you are. Each day we are stuffed with more adverts and promos urging us to get this latest designer watch or those trendy new shoes. It's a cycle that never seems to end. A lot of us spend time chasing after these things, blinded and convinced they'll provide us with the happiness we need. I have been there and I can tell you that these shiny new objects do not give you the happiness they promise.

Here is my own simple definition of minimalism,

## Minimalism & Decluttering

*Minimalism is a form of intentional living that allows you to reassess your priorities and reconsider what truly brings value to your life. Minimalism strips you off distractions and allows you to reconnect with what brings you freedom.*

As you read on, you may want to tweak this definition to better encapsulate your experience. Wants and needs vary from person to person. It's likely that minimalism achieves your needs in a different way.

## Minimalism vs. the Culture of Consumerism

There's no way to sugarcoat it: we live in an obnoxiously consumerist culture. The pressure to consume is so strong that everywhere you look there's a new billboard shoving an attractive product in your face. Just walking outside can incite a battle of the mind and urges.

Being influenced by culture is normal, but some aspects of this culture can be quite damaging if care is not taken. Consumerism and minimalism are two opposing forces in modern day. The ultimate victor depends wholly on you. Every day, these large companies shell out millions of dollars in search of your attention. Social media influencers who act as their minions are also intent on getting you to consume more. The dominant message sent with these ads is, "You need to buy this product. Wealthy and attractive people all around the world use this product – and don't you want to be like them?"

Advertisements are crafted daily with this intended message in mind. But ask yourself, "Did I need this before I saw the advertisement? Or do I only need it now that I know it exists? Is this need real or is a company trying to make me feel this way?" These are the basics of minimalism. It starts with the mind. It starts with talking to and cautioning yourself. No one is saying you should not be influenced by YouTube or Facebook ads, but learn to probe the intention of the sellers. What do they really want from you? Will this product offer value to you or does a company just want your money?

## 8 Life-Altering Benefits of Minimalism

There are many obvious benefits of decluttering, such as having a more organized home, but the benefits of minimalism go much deeper than that. Here are some of the biggest benefits of minimalism:

### 1. Emotional Stability and Clarity of Mind

The connection between the mind and the number of possessions we own is a strong one. Research has shown that a few minutes a day to clear out the trash, make the bed and deal with the laundry can massively impact our mental state and provide peace of mind. When we're not surrounded by mess, we subconsciously relax. When there aren't a million tiny objects to distract us, we can think more clearly and make better decisions.

### 2. Reduced Stress

Knowing that once you walk into your home, you'll find a pile of clothes on the bedroom floor, plates in the sink and books littered on the dining table is enough to make a lot of people fear the doorknob. It can create a psychological drain and if you're not careful with it, depression may even set in. Clutter eats up space in your home and can create a sense of claustrophobia, a feeling that your own home is being taken over. You must deal with clutter before it chases you out of your own home.

### 3. More Room for Things of Value

As I've illustrated, less is more. When you purge your life and flush out the things that aren't important, you are creating more space for things of value. As long as your life is filled with junk, there will never be space for what you really need. I don't just mean in terms of physical space, but also financially. If you're spending all your income on new clothes, how are you ever going to afford a comfortable new sofa? Call me crazy but I think it's much better to own three pairs of quality socks than a hundred torn ones.

### 4. Better Relationships

Minimalist principles apply to all aspects of our lives, and that includes our personal relationships. When we practice minimalism on a deep level, we become a magnet for better friendships and relationships. You see, even certain people in our lives can be considered 'excess.' How many of your friendships truly bring value to your life? Who are you only friends with because you want to seem more popular? Minimalism teaches us that having few but close connections is better than having many impersonal acquaintances.

### 5. Improved Time Management

Clutter kills time. Have you ever searched for a bunch of keys in a disorganized desk? No one wants to go through that on a busy morning. Clutter is a beast that can eat into your time. We waste a lot of time searching through needless junk for the items we really need. Think of how much time we'd save if we didn't have to endure this confusion!

### 6. A Happier Planet

The earth is at the mercy of your minimalism. Less clutter in our homes means less waste in landfills and in the oceans. A lot of our clutter cannot be recycled. If we continue to purchase clutter, companies will only continue to produce it. And let's face it, we don't need most of these shiny objects. If you live a minimalist life, you can go on with a clearer conscience. You can rest easier knowing you are not contributing to the world's growing trash pile.

### 7. Sense of Purpose

Motivation can return to your life after the process of decluttering. It is almost like you are starting life all over, like you have been reborn, giving yourself a second chance. Once you have gotten clutter out of the way, confusion leaves and a sense of clarity sets in. I have often heard people say that once they lose motivation or interest for a certain activity they stop for a while and clear their surroundings. There's nothing like the beauty that comes with the creation of space. It's a good way to remind yourself of the control you have over your life.

## 8. Emotional Freedom

Emotional freedom comes when we learn to let go of emotional clutter. We accumulate emotional clutter when we hold onto feelings such as malice, jealousy, grudges, and hatred. When you find the strength to settle scores, pay off debt and move on from mistakes, your mind is relieved. When we hold grudges or feel jealous of someone, this exhausts our emotional system. Imagine what you could have accomplished with that energy if you hadn't lost it to such negativity.

## The Relationship between Minimalism and Decluttering

As I explained in my introduction, minimalism and decluttering are two capsules used together to cure the clutter disease. People use both words interchangeably thinking that they mean the same thing. This is an understandable mistake. Although they cover the same concepts, they are not the same. One serves as a springboard leading to the achievement of the other.

Decluttering is the beginning process for people who want to take back their lives and own their spaces. Some people who indulge in decluttering have no intention of living a minimalist life. For them it is just about decluttering today, waiting for the clutter to accumulate again, then decluttering again. For them decluttering is a form of therapy, a way to clean up their lives on a temporary note. As a whole, decluttering is hardly a life changing process. It is just like brushing your teeth every day or vacuuming the sitting room each morning. The result of decluttering is often never permanent. Most people often go back to decluttering every other month or year.

Minimalism and decluttering both share the same theme, which is the removal and disposal of excesses in one's life. Decluttering consists of a simple process while minimalism is an adopted lifestyle. Minimalism is a mindset where the practitioner has committed to only having things of value and importance in their lives. Minimalism helps to curb the excesses of consumerism so that decluttering will not be needed. It is all about living and surviving with less so that more intangible rewards can be attained.

# The Warning Signs Signaling Clutter that You Cannot Ignore

Clutter is an ever-increasing monster, but the only problem with this monster is that you never notice its growth until the day it jumps out of the closet and grabs you by the neck. Just like a sickness, not everyone sees it coming. Study these signs and compare them with what's going on in your home right now.

1. **You're Overwhelmed in Your Own Personal Space and Private Life**

In my years of experience dealing with clutter, I can say that this is probably the most dangerous sign of all. It manifests itself in small ways. You wake up in the morning and remember all the appointments you have for the day and instantly begin to feel overwhelmed even before getting out of bed. Frustration sets in and the essence and joy of life is lost.

Once you get home, it seems like your own house has locked you out, even though you have the keys. You discover piles of confusing items that keep jeering their faces at you. You become confused and pray earnestly for the next morning so you can run away from the mess in your own home. Guess what? Clutter in the home is equal to clutter in the mind. Your home is yours and yours alone and you have to deal with it one way or another.

2. **A Distracted and Unfocused Mind**

All monsters are unattractive and they can easily cause distractions when they arrive. No one can remain calm in the presence of a gorilla-sized humanoid with horns and razor-sharp fangs. That is how it is with clutter as well; you can't get anything done in its presence because it causes one to feel scattered and unfocused. Even seemingly minor clutter like unwashed dishes can create anxiety and steal away focus. Clutter isn't only a hindrance to productivity, it can also get in the way of relaxation.

3. **Buying to Impress**

If you often feel tempted to buy particular items because you want to impress family and friends, even when you don't really like these products and may not need them, know that you are living a cluttered life. Chances are that most of the other things you own were bought with this mindset and are creating clutter in your home. Anytime you are forced to seek validation from an outside source other than yourself, the happiness you find will be shallow and never fulfilling.

### 4. You Have Trouble Finding Things

Clutter swallows things up. When this happens, you'll have to beg this monster to release your things back to you. Have you ever wondered why you can't find the T.V remote, or your socks, or even a screwdriver when you actually need it? The answer is simple: clutter. These things have lost their rightful places in your home.

Books under the bed, spoons in the living room, knitting needles stuffed between the cushions: if any of this brings your home to mind, then you need to declutter. If you find yourself constantly misplacing things, then it's possible you own too much stuff. Once all extraneous items are cleared away, it immediately becomes easier to find items in the home.

### 5. You Own a Junk Drawer

Junk drawers are gradually becoming common in today's world, and this is a result of people having far too much stuff. The junk drawer is a dumping ground for miscellaneous items. Frankly, you do not need a junk drawer. If you can't find a home for certain possessions, then you should honestly rethink their necessity. As its name suggests, most of the objects placed in this drawer are junk.

### 6. You're Ashamed of Your space

Does the thought of a friend coming over to visit you send shivers down your spine? Do you start frantically cleaning and tidying when someone calls to say they are coming over for a brief visit? If you answered 'yes' to these questions, you likely have a big clutter problem. Let's get to work on it right away before clutter becomes the landlord and you become the tenant.

# CHAPTER TWO - LAYING THE FOUNDATION FOR YOUR BEST MINIMALIST SELF

Powerful Principles to Help You See the World as a True Minimalist

To reap the full benefit of minimalism, you must be willing to pay the price mentally, psychologically and physically. As we've established in the previous chapter, minimalism doesn't just deal with the physical aspect of your life; minimalism goes deeper, penetrating one's mindset and attitude towards life. These following principles will help you prepare yourself for the journey ahead of you.

### 1. Your Possessions Don't Define You

Contrary to what most people believe, you are not what you own. Your possessions do not define your worth and value. Unfortunately, many people make purchases with this misconception in mind. If you want to look good, go ahead, and if you want the latest accessories, go for it, but don't make these purchases with desperation. And do so without accumulating clutter.

It is not easy to practice minimalism in the world we live in today. We are constantly reminded of how we could and should be wealthier. We are bombarded by messages telling us the more we have, the more attractive, worthy, and interesting we are. But how many times have the products we've bought delivered on these promises? At the end of the day, we still have the same insecurities and the same obstacles. Chances are, even when you bought what you thought would be a quick-fix to something, you continued to encounter that problem. Your possessions will not fix what you're unhappy with. How much you own does not determine your worth. This may be a sign that you don't feel fulfilled in your life; once you chase what truly makes you happy, and allow yourself to be defined by your accomplishments, you will no longer need material objects.

## 2. See your possessions for what they truly are

It is time to take a bold step and honestly assess all your possessions. Look around your home and observe what's creating clutter. Ask yourself why you spent so much time and energy acquiring, maintaining and storing all these objects. The stuff we own can be divided into any of the following categories: functional objects, beautifying items, and sentimental things.

Functional objects get certain jobs done. They are needed to help us carry out everyday activities. Some of these are essential for our survival while others exist simply to make our lives better. It is important you understand that not everything you want is necessary for your survival. You might like to believe that, but it isn't the truth. Any functional objects that make day-to-day living easier are welcome in your new minimalist world. A home can function just fine in the absence of a skateboard but cannot do the same in the absence of cooking pots. Both things add value to a home, but the value of one outshines the other.

Beautifying items are brought into the home because they add aesthetic value to their surroundings. Art should be appreciated and embraced since this can sometimes add ambiance or a sense of calm to a room. But be careful as too many beautifying items can still form clutter, especially color clutter. Observe your shelf for a while and notice the presence of mismatched antiques. Just because you appreciated that sculpted object a few months after your mother's death does not mean that it should have a lifelong space in your home. We outgrow things and our love for them, and that is completely normal.

Things that do not fall into any of the previously mentioned categories usually turn out to have sentimental value. These can consist of gifts, inherited belongings, or objects that remind you of a particular point in your life. Sentimental objects remind you of the places you have been, the people you met along the way and the experiences you had.

When assessing your belongings, answer these questions:

- What value does this add to my home?
- Would I consider replacing this if it ever gets broken or lost, or would I be relieved it was finally out my hands?
- Did I need this item before I acquired it?

3. **The joy of simple living**

When you simplify your life, you are left with the basic, most necessary things that give you value and joy. Limit your purchases and acquisitions to the bare minimum so that you allow only what you need into your life. Having only the essentials in your home is a major component of minimalism. Doing so helps to prevent the influx of domestic waste (which is a form of clutter in itself). Strive to reduce your consumption rate so that you only have the things you need to satisfy your immediate needs.

Most consumers in our modern world can't even take comprehensive stock of the things they own because they own so much. Simple living helps you to stay aware of and responsible for your possessions. Perhaps you asked yourself one morning, "Where is my navy-blue polo shirt?" And even after weeks of searching you were unable to locate it. That is one major sign of clutter. You own things that you do not need or use and this has given birth to irresponsibility.

4. **Crave the availability of space**

Every once in a while, we just want to have a breath of fresh air. Have you ever tried doing that in a room full of other people? Of course not, because it brings no comfort. In fact, the room full of people is likely why you need that breath of fresh air. You'll find yourself breathing in cologne and body odor. It would be different if that space was clear. Naturally, we all feel calmer in an empty, clear space.

The absence of space causes distress. When there isn't enough of it, claustrophobia begins to eat you up. Many people believe their space problem can only be solved by moving to a larger house or compound. Within a few months of arrival, however, the clutter begins to form again on this new environment. Don't run away from your lack of space; tackle it head on and start creating more space. This is what minimalism helps you achieve. Every space becomes enough for you because you have mastered the art of creating more whenever you need it.

As I established in my introduction, clutter is a monster that eats up space. One day you wake up and discover that all the space you once enjoyed has disappeared and you wonder what happened. It was a gradual process and because space is silent, it uttered no word as it was being swallowed. Don't fret over your lost space. You might have lost it as fast as a finger snap but it is not lost forever. All you have to do is get rid of needless belongings.

You must take into consideration the amount of space you have in your home before buying more stuff. Remember that the space in your home is not emptiness. It brings its own aesthetic value. It allows all who live in that space to breathe easier and freer. Learn to crave this feeling, instead of stuff.

### 5. Less stuff means less stress

People rarely consider this, but it takes a lot of physical and mental energy to manage all the stuff you own. After purchasing the item and that fleeting moment of what I call the 'buyer's high,' the fun of the situation begins to go steadily downhill. Not only does this item now take up space in your home, but you must expend energy keeping it in place and out of the way. And should the item break, it'll cost more money and time to have it repaired. Soon, it begins to feel like the products control your life, instead of the other way around.

The stress attached to accumulating possessions comes in stages. A sense of alienation and deprivation sets in once you discover that you don't own a particular item. "Gosh! I'm so out of style!" you might find yourself thinking. This is when stress begins to develop. There's a sense of feeling irrelevant if you don't own the right product. Then there is the stress related to acquiring the item. You start window shopping, surfing the web, and scrolling aimlessly through Amazon. Soon, you have an increased heart rate.

You realize you can't quite afford the item, but you put it out of your mind and buy it anyway. Your excitement outweighs your rational mind, but the stress seeps in once you click that 'confirm purchase' button. When the item arrives, you're filled with that familiar euphoria, but this doesn't last long. Once it loses its shine, it ends up in the same corner with all the other things you once loved, but that no longer interest you. It becomes another thing to throw out of the way when you can't find what you need.

Take a moment to remember life before you owned so many possessions. Everything was a whole lot simpler. You possessed that unadulterated joy of a minimalist, and probably more money, too.

I'm not trying to convince you to live in the woods, feeding on slugs and earthworms, with only a bed of hay and a wooden spoon. I'm only asking you to reflect. Imagine yourself without half of the possessions you currently own. Consider your life without your entire mug selection or the books you've owned for years but have never read. Consider your life if you only owned the handbags and purses you *actually* use. Chances are, your life is not any worse. And think of all the stress you'd be removing from your life!

## 6. **Contentment is powerful**

I can't stress this point enough: contentment is the foundation upon which a minimalist lifestyle is built. A greedy person or hoarder will never be able to practice minimalism to the fullest, unless they undergo a complete transformation. What's crazy about the modern world is that most of us *are* content with the things we already own – until we're harassed by the idea that something better exists and told we need to buy it now.

Once your basic needs as a human being are taken care of, then happiness should be in place. Your happiness should not be dependent on the things you own; when that happens, happiness becomes unattainable. When you learn to appreciate the little you have, you begin to see abundance in everything and life becomes even more enjoyable. Focus on what you have instead of what you don't have, because once you begin to compare your life with the lives of people around you, your hunger for more stuff never rests. Stuff cannot fill the void of your deep discontentment and dissatisfaction.

You must practice the art of believing that you have enough before you actually have enough. 'Enough' is, after all, a thing of the mind in the modern age when most of us have our basic needs satisfied very easily. It all has to do with self-control and self-discipline.

### 7. Protect the flow of things into your life

How easy is it for useless things to get into your life and settle there? Everyday more consumables pop up in search of a new home, and unless you practice self-awareness, your home is at risk of inviting this new clutter in. Protecting the flow of things into your life means you should only allow things of value in – the things that provide you with undiluted joy, free from the need to please or make others approve of you.

These clutter-building objects do not have legs or wings. We must ask ourselves, "How do they find their way into our homes?" Either we buy them or they are gifted to us.

Your home is your personal space; it is the only part of the whole world where you can be king or queen. A conscious effort must be made to protect the home from these unwanted materials. Before anything finds its way into your home, assess your entire situation.

The necessary questions here include:

- What role do I see this object playing, if any, in a few months' time?
- Is there a place in my life for this item right now?
- What is motivating me to purchase this?

- How long has it been since I purchased something that functions the same way?

You may be wondering, "But what do I do about gifts, giveaways, or freebies?" Politely refusing an item sometimes works fine, but most people don't have the mind to do that because of their relationship with the giver. If you truly feel you need to collect that item, go ahead, but make a mental note to take that item out of its place in a few months, and have it discarded, donated or sold. Don't allow this clutter to settle down in your home. Your home is not a dumpster.

## 8. Live life free from the shackles of Possessions

The best minimalists are those who have learned to manage the effects that possessions have on their well-being. The idea here is to loosen the grip that your belongings have on your identity. The emotional strongholds that we build around these objects can be binding and if we aren't careful, they may lead to suffering. Detaching from your belongings means finding emotional freedom, looking beyond the monetary value of possessions to see the real value of life.

The benefits of practicing detachment from possessions are numerous and life-altering. This will eventually lead to a less greedy personality. When you are no longer plagued by an insatiable hunger for stuff, you will find far more life satisfaction. You can finally find freedom from the material hang-ups of the modern world. Have you ever heard of families ruined by conflict over who gets to inherit a recently deceased loved-one's stuff? That doesn't have to be you!

Minimalism is a wakeup call to stop feeling defined by your belongings and to form attachments with aspects of life that create deeper joy. Help out in the community. There are new experiences beckoning to you. There are numerous people you can meet and forge new relationships with.

Although we might want to shy away from the topic of death, it will befall us all at some point. When your time comes, all the useless items you've become attached to will be left behind and serve no purpose.

The things you leave behind will be what you're remembered for. While preparing for your minimalist life, take a few moments to sort through your belongings and consider what impression this will leave. This is not to make you fear or worry about death, but to make you understand that only a few things in your life are actually worth the space they occupy.

9. **You don't have to own it to enjoy it**

Consider this question: why do you have to own it to enjoy it? Adding a new object to your pile of clutter is not the only way you get to experience the benefits of that object. In this day and age, we are so eager to own things (and sometimes, even people) which we can call ours and *only* ours – but this is a silly way of living life. Items that are communal in some way are just as good. By borrowing or renting an item, you can still make good use of it without ever having to worry about its long-term place in your home. If you need a new book, why not borrow one from a friend or the library? If you need an outfit for a fancy event, there are many companies offering rentals of high-end clothing for short-term use. Rentals are much cheaper than purchases. Not only is this kinder to your wallet, it's also kinder to your home.

## Everyday Minimalist Habits to Get You In the Zone

You probably knew this already, but minimalism isn't just a habit, it's also a lifestyle. For die-hard minimalists, it can even seem like a religion. For a little humor, consider clutter as the evil of this minimalist 'religion.' Just as every other religion has its everyday rituals to help followers stay connected to its teachings, minimalism also has its own routines and habits that serve a similar purpose.

There are simple habits that should be implemented daily or weekly into your new minimalist schedule. These habits may seem small but they'll create a world of difference. Most of these daily rituals can be carried out in mere seconds, without eating up too much of your time. Before we get into the habits of minimalism, let me explain a great strategy for integrating healthy new habits into your life.

- **A life hack for developing better habits**

When we try to create better habits, we tend to make things hard on ourselves. It doesn't have to be this way. Want to know a secret? You should find a way to attach the habits you want to develop to already existing habits. If listening to podcasts is part of your daily schedule, try doing this *while* doing something you don't enjoy as much. You could attach this habit to the less-enjoyable act of washing the dishes. Or you could connect the habit of getting ready for bed with the practice of clearing your desk space. When it comes to creating new habits, this is a tried-and-true way of making them stick.

# MINIMALIST HABITS

## 1. Fire up your minimalist mindset every day

Start each day by reading or watching anything that has to do with minimalism. This way, you can ensure you always stay motivated. Refreshing your mindset about the powerful benefits of minimalism will help to keep you on track, especially on days you feel like giving up. Do it first thing in the morning because that is when your subconscious is most active and receptive to information.

Almost every ad on social media or TV is a promotion of consumerism. The more you pay attention to them the more you find yourself drifting away from minimalist teachings. Be diligent as you adopt this new lifestyle. Make a conscious effort to fill your morning, and in essence, your day with information that matters and information that will benefit you. Subscribe to minimalism channels on YouTube and follow minimalism influencers on Instagram. Start every day by revving your minimalist engine.

## 2. Find your tribe

The people you spend time with will inevitably influence your actions. You can't nurture a minimalist dream while hanging out with materialistic people. One party will influence the other, and I'll tell you now, materialism is far more catching than minimalism. No matter how disciplined you are as a minimalist, it will take a great deal of emotional and mental energy to not get sucked back into a world of consumerism.

If the people in your life live in alignment with minimalist teachings, it will be easier to make this new lifestyle stick for good. Minimalism will no longer be something you have to *try* to embody; it will simply be the new norm. You will not think otherwise. This is why it's important to find your tribe. This doesn't mean you can't socialize or get to know any other people (obviously!), it just means you need to be aware of who you surround yourself with and how that will impact your new life changes. Evaluate your life now and consider which people will be good and which ones will be bad for your promising new chapter. Come up with methods that will protect you from their materialistic ways if you ever need to hang out with each other.

### 3. Gratitude

Gratitude is powerful. Gratitude energizes the smile on your face and makes you the most attractive person in the room. This habit is easy to incorporate into your day, but as I've said, you will need a drastic change of mindset. The only difference between a grateful and ungrateful person is their mindset. Once you start looking at the world through the lens of gratitude, you instantly feel far happier.

Every morning, just before your kids or partner are awake, take out your special notebook or journal and list out three things you are grateful for. This can be anything! Your kid scored 80% on a pop quiz after you helped them study? Show gratitude for being blessed with a smart child. Is it a cold, wet, and miserable time of year? Show gratitude for having shelter from such terrible weather. Just think, you could be out there in the freezing cold right now! Contentment is only a thought away when you make gratitude a daily habit.

### 4. Fill your life with experiences, not stuff

Value the experiences and memories that life brings your way. People will not remember you for the things you brought home from the mall, but for the experiences that you gave them while you were with them. Go somewhere fun. Go see a waterfall and experience the beauty. Cook someone a fantastic dinner. Shared memories and experiences are the rock on which friendships and relationships are built. People will always remember you for how you made them feel.

### 5. Learn to say "no" when necessary

Never underestimate the power of saying 'no.' Despite how small the word is, it carries a lot of weight and power. Lives have been changed and saved just because someone dared to say 'no.' As a minimalist, you have to cultivate the habit of saying no whenever it needs to be said. Saying no doesn't make you a mean person. In fact, it's saying yes when you shouldn't or when you don't mean it that makes you a coward. Do you find yourself unable to say no to people? Do these people always end up coming back? It's probably because they know they'll never be refused by you. Look around, some of the most respected members of society are those that say no at the right time. They are not easily swayed into other people's schedules and plans.

The habit of saying no can be learned with constant practice and over time. Saying no to others is saying yes to yourself and releasing yourself from future engagements and commitments which may turn out to be clutter in your schedule. Or worse, your bank account.

Say no to the kids who might want extra toys. Say no to friends who might want you to host a party even if you don't have the time and resources to do so. Say no even to your own self, when you mind is begging you to buy a new novel at the bookstore when there are a hundred in your home library that you haven't even opened.

### 6. Plan a simple but nutritious meal

Simplifying your meals will teach your taste buds and overall palate to enjoy and accept the natural taste of food. The need to add extra flavoring to your meals will be reduced. This lifestyle change will prevent more packaging from finding its way into your home. A constant attempt to outdo yourself in the kitchen can be a drain on your time and energy. Have a meal plan that can be easily repeated with variety from time to time. Your shopping process will turn out to be much more streamlined and clutter will be far more controlled.

### 7. Employ space control mechanisms

Creating more space in your home is a decent way to deal with clutter, but it's not the best way. What you may have only succeeded in doing is providing more space for the growth of clutter. Instead of looking for how to create space in your home, employ mechanisms that will help you control the space that you already own. People have been building increasingly large homes and yet clutter still exists. Once we see the availability of space, it is our human nature to want to fill it up with stuff. For minimalism to take full effect, we must learn to suppress this urge.

Have two boxes placed at strategic points in your home. These boxes are for possessions that you are making up your mind to let go of. One of them will contain the things you want to sell or donate and the other will contain things that you want to discard. With that settled, stay alert and aware of what's eating up space in your home. Identify the things that have lost their value in your home and choose to either donate or discard them. This simple trick works wonders and clears up space within months of continuous practice.

## 8. Minimize your debt

Debt is a form of clutter on its own. It weighs you down both emotionally, financially and in your relationships with people. It may not work in exactly the same way as material clutter, but debt accumulated over time will always come with frustration, anger and depression. Minimalist philosophies stress the importance of preventing the creation of debt, but in the event that it has already happened, you must make plans to pay it all off and remove the burden.

Don't fret. It might seem like an insurmountable giant, but a step by step approach will nail it in the head. First, make up your mind to not accumulate more debt. Before you call your friends to ask for a loan or worse, buy something expensive on your credit card, consider deeply if it is necessary. Most times we fall into debt just because we're so convinced we'll get our act together later. If you can't do it now, why will later be any better?

Do some calculations and figure out what your weekly or monthly income is. From that sum you can set out a certain percentage for paying off debt, bit by bit. If you can make the payments automatic or a direct reduction from your paycheck, do it. It will also help to develop emergency funds; in other words, money you can fall back on when the time arises. Set up an account and send small chunks of your earnings into this account. Save money in this account over time and resist all urges to spend from it, unless you absolutely have no other choice and desperately need the money. No, your 'wants' do not count!

### 9. Go for quality every single time

They say anything worth doing at all is worth doing well. I say, "Anything worth buying at all is worth buying in high quality." Substandard goods always turn out to be cheap because the sellers are sure that they won't last long in your possession. When we catch sight of these low prices, however, we find it hard to resist making the purchase. Inevitably, wear and tear occurs and you return to buy a new set of these same substandard products. Over time a growing pile of low-quality products appears in your home, when you could have just bought one high-quality product instead. Not only is this a waste of space, in the long run it's also a waste of money. Don't be fooled by that cheap price tag! Quality comes with the extra cost and your peace of mind is worth that extra cost.

# CHAPTER THREE - DECLUTTER YOUR HOME 101

Now it's time to get into the minimalist decluttering process in real detail. We have successfully established the foundations of minimalism, the importance of minimalism, and the habits that will set you on the right track towards a life of unrestricted freedom from material objects. This chapter will walk you through essential decluttering processes. Like everything we've demonstrated so far, it's vital that you make these practices part of your routine, and not just a one-time activity.

## Light Decluttering: How do I start?

One of the most significant drawbacks of starting any new habit or task is figuring out where on earth to begin. When decluttering the home, there is always a place to start. When you look around your home and see clutter lying around your living room or your bedroom floor, something speaks to you and says: "You can't do this. It is too much. Where will you put all of this stuff?" Don't get worked up and overwhelmed by fear. All you need to do is adopt consistency. Decluttering doesn't happen in an instant. It is a process that takes time because it also took some time to build up. As you take time to practice it more and more, you begin to get better and better at it. Soon you find yourself naturally engaging in the process. It has become part of you.

The key to decluttering from scratch is to take everything out of its designated place. Turn the drawers upside down and pour out all its contents. Strip down the closet to bare hooks, rods, and shelving. Don't forget that you will need a free space to dump out the things to be either discarded or donated. I suggest you start with one small area at a time so that the room you are presently working on does not become crowded with materials and hinder free movement.

Pretend that you're starting life in your home all over again. Seeing belongings in a different place will change your perspective about its arrangement. And pouring out your stuff can help you identify some items that haven't been in their proper place for a while. Don't hesitate to take anything out of its designated space. Pick a portion of the house you are most comfortable with and start. There are many places you can begin decluttering, and no single one is better than the other. It can be your bedroom, or the attic or the basement. Just pick a spot. When you are there, you can look for a smaller portion of it and work on that: under the bed space, the wardrobe or the shoe rack. Don't neglect any part of it because every overlooked corner holds clutter that can grow if you don't pay attention.

## Tips to Maintain a Permanently Decluttered Home

1. **What stays and what goes:** Once you have poured out clutter from its hiding place, you need to start the sorting process. This is the point at which you must find the root cause of all your clutter. The sorting process has three categories: Keep, Discard, and Donate. You will need three containers for each of these. Boxes will also work well to help you out, mostly, if you need to deal with smaller items. If you have a smaller box, you can use it for things that you have presently not made up your mind about. As you sort through, you will come across items that have you pausing and feeling confused about whether to throw them or keep them. Throw them into the box and go back to them later so they don't slow down your progress.

The possibility of you finishing up with boxes full of undecided materials is very high. You don't have to fret. Seal it up and place a date on it with a marker. Give the items some time and come back to sort through them again. By this time, you will have a clearer mind and judgment about the future of these belongings in your life. You should not get too entangled in the decision of having a box full of undecided items. That is a form of clutter on its own. Don't just dump it in the basement and forget it because you feel that you do not have the emotional stamina to let go of those things. The point here isn't to find a different storage place for these items, but to keep the decluttering process as fast and smooth as possible.

☐ **The discard box:** The content of this box can be called the 'Discardables.' Don't linger on the name, as these items are basically trash. These items serve no purpose in your life. Don't get carried away and do not drop any of them into the 'Keep' box. The truth should always prevail in your decision-making. There are things you might feel still have value but inside of your heart you know they are trash; you just don't want to let them go because they hold certain memories or ideas about what you want to be. The discard box is filled with things that are hard to let go of. If it cannot be fixed, then you should let go of it.

Recycling some of these items is an option. Have your immediate environment in mind as you sort through these items. Go on YouTube and search for information about stuff that can easily be recycled for a greater purpose and value. Proper disposal of trash should be an important consideration as you sort through the pile. Where will these things end up? What can be repurposed and reused?

☐ **The Keep Box:** This will contain all the things that you want to keep. The possessions here will include everything that still brings value to your household and life, things you truly cherish, and things that are still functional and useful. If you haven't used some items in years then you should know that they don't belong in that box. They will be more useful in a donation box or in the box of undecided items.

☐ **The donation box:** This box will contain items which are still useful but no longer serve any purpose for you. Examples are the expensive toys lying around the basement, despite your youngest child already being in high school. You can give them out to new parents. They will have more value in their home than it will have in yours. Don't feel bad about letting them go. You are giving yourself freedom,

## Minimalism & Decluttering

and you are providing those items with a new life where they will be more appreciated. Something will keep speaking to you saying, "But you might still need this someday." Resist the urge to succumb to that thought. If you don't need it today, the possibility that you will need some other day is very slim.

Be more generous with the items in your donation pile. Rest assured knowing that someone out there will appreciate them. You might also be worried about where to take your donations. There are numerous religious organizations that are always in need of materials to give out to the less privileged. The Red Cross and other medical organizations accept your donations to deliver in relief of IDP camps around the world. All you need to do is carry out a little research on the internet, and the right people will come knocking at your door to help you take out your donations.

If you are reluctant to release your belongings to the world this way, then consider selling them instead. The cash will provide you with more value than the item lying around the house. Hold a garage or yard sale. You will be amazed by the amount of money you can make from one. There are a variety of things you can sell, from books to CDs, DVDs to golfing equipment. You will be shocked by how many people in your vicinity desperately need the stuff you have been hoarding.

**2. A purpose for each item:** It is very easy for the 'Keep' box to become flooded with items. Before any item should be taken back into your home and life, it is necessary that you reassess its true importance in your life. Ask yourself the essential question about each item you come across. Each item in your 'Keep' box should be making a noticeable positive contribution to your life. Everything else should not go in this box.

While you're going through these objects, you'll come across many things that serve exactly the same purpose. They may have different decoration or packaging, but they ultimately do the same thing. This is a case of duplication, and it should be appropriately handled and taken care of. Minimalism is about clearing excess from your life. Some of these items in the home can easily multiply and clog up drawers. Examples are pens, paper clips, or buttons. Save a reasonable quantity and do away with the rest of them.

Other items that aren't in the class of duplicated items should now be scrutinized. Probe the essence of each item, figuring out its value and how much that value is needed in your home.

The answers that come to your mind will guide you on where to place the items, either in a donation box or in a 'Keep' box. Some items might have some form of value, but the space they will provide once they are taken out of the way might be more valuable. Provide yourself with that new space and get that object out of the way.

While sorting through and making categorizations, you could consider having an objective and responsible friend who is also a minimalist around you. Their presence will provide you with enough drive to do the right thing. Having to explain why you want to keep one stupid item or the other can be embarrassing. You will look through your belongings with clearer eyes and understand why you need to let go of them.

While going through your stuff, keep in mind that you only make use of 30% or less of the things you own every month. And the difference is hardly ever noticed. Some of the things you hoard and protect so dearly will serve no purpose in your life throughout the year. But because there is space, you just decide to house them. Be more rigid during your sorting process. Look for the essentials that make up the less-than-30% and keep them. These are your most important possessions.

**3. A home for everything:** In your own home, each of your possessions should have their own homes - space they will occupy from now on. It should be at the core of your minimalist mindset: everything should have its place. It is an important principle of minimalism. It's much easier for you to keep stock and prevent stray items from moving into your home when there are designated places for everything. When this is in place, it is easier for you to identify things that should not be in your home and things that don't belong in your environment.

There are considerations to be made while making these designations, some of which include frequency of usage, size, fragility, and proximity. The house is already broken down into smaller units of rooms. Sometimes, if one is lucky or rich enough, the various rooms are broken down into smaller compartments or spaces to contain some special class of possessions or items. For example, cupboards in the kitchen can hold ceramics and cooking utensils, and walk-in-closets in the room can hold all clothes. An item's home should generally be closest to the place where it is most needed. If you have any clothes lying in a pile on your bathroom floor, it's time to move them to the place where they are needed.

The things you use most frequently are to be kept closest to you in a place where you can easily reach them. You will want to be able to access these items without unnecessarily scavenging and rummaging through your other stuff.

Once you have identified and designated a place for everything, it will help to label each of these places so that anyone coming into your home will know exactly where to put things after using them. Use it as a sort of address for each item. Even your kids will get used to it and follow this simple instruction. Get your family members actively involved in the decluttering process. If everyone has a mindset of decluttering and minimalism, it will be easier to tackle this monster. A collaborative effort does wonders. Clothes should be hung instead of piled on boxes or chairs. Take the utensils back to their hanging spaces instead of leaving them on the kitchen counter. Return books back to the shelf instead of leaving them on floors or chairs.

Once you come into a room, try to find items that aren't in their places and return them home. It will only take you a few minutes out of the hours of the day and the huge difference will be noticed in your household.

**4. Keep clear surfaces** - Wide and flat surfaces are major breeding grounds for clutter. Most items will end up on clear surfaces, there's no doubt about it. Take a look around your house. Surfaces like the dining table, kitchen counters or living room coffee table are likely loaded with clutter. This will build up gradually until the whole surface has been colonized by junk.

Clear surfaces add a certain kind of beauty to any environment that surrounds them. They offer endless possibilities. The clear surface in the kitchen will help you prepare a quick meal without any hindrance. A decluttered dining table will accommodate members of a family for breakfast. The importance of clear surfaces cannot be overemphasized. We don't realize the value of a clear surface until we find one covered in clutter. Suddenly, we can't put a single plate down, or we have nowhere to put our laptop down for work.

To ensure your surfaces stay clear, you must adopt a new attitude and observe some basic decluttering principles. Your surfaces should not be used as storage spaces. By all means necessary, your surfaces should be kept clean and clear at all times. These steps will help you:

i. Clear off every single object on that flat surface. Whether they should be on the surface or not is irrelevant at this early stage. They will be returned later, if they belong here.
ii. Once the surface is clear, stand back from it and notice the calm that comes with having a clear surface. See how inviting the surface is, observe the beauty of space.
iii. Identify what purpose that surface serves in your home. Is it a surface that serves a specific function (such as a kitchen counter) or is it used during moments of creativity? Maybe you want to use it for something totally different from its former purpose. Once you have successfully identified its function, you can now determine what will be going back on the surface and what shouldn't be on the surface.

iv. Try not to allow more than three objects on any table. Anything more than that will constitute as clutter. If it's an essential object, put it on a shelf or anywhere else closeby. Allow surfaces to remain as clear as possible until the habit sticks.

v. You can add up to two additional items for aesthetic value on these surfaces. These will serve to complement the surface and keep it from looking too bare or boring.

It is one thing to achieve a clear surface and it is another thing to keep it cleared. A lot of people clear up surfaces every day, but before the day is over they are back to square one. These tips will help you keep your surfaces cleared for a longer period of time.

- **Drop your items on the floor when you get home.** It is a basic instinct to drop things that come with you into a room on a clean and clear surface. It is relaxing to get the weight off your hands and onto a clear table or counter. Then they sit there for hours or days, neglected because they are not in your way. The most important rule is to get nothing on the surface in the first place, place those items on the floor and once they make you trip twice, you'll be eager to finally put them in their designated place. It might seem too extreme for you, but minimalism has to be extreme sometimes, especially if you are a person that easily gets comfortable with clutter. Discipline yourself against clutter. With time, you will notice an attitude shift that has you organizing anything you come home with at all times.

- **Wipe surfaces down at least twice every week.** Wiping surfaces down draws your attention to the clutter growing on them. As you wipe, put away whatever shouldn't be on the surface and move aside anything that gets in the way of your cleaning. Discard any trash or useless pieces of junk and return the surface back to its initial glory. Do this at least twice every week.

- **Leave nothing for later.** When you're in the process of clearing things away, it can be tempting to tell yourself you'll finish off certain tasks later. Don't do this. If you're done folding the clothes, send them over to the closet immediately. Don't leave them on the ironing table. You were reading a book at the dining table when you realized you had to pick the kids up from school. Send that book over to the shelf before you leave the house. This is a major key to leaving surfaces as clear as they should be. Adopt the habit of putting things away as soon as you are done with them. Once you get used to this, the house can almost clear itself.

- **Prevent the accumulation of small clutter.** We are all guilty of letting 'small clutter' build up in our homes. You notice it growing but you never quite recognize it as clutter until one eye-opening day. As the name suggests, small clutter consists of smaller items, such as pens, paperclips, or useless little knick-knacks. It takes a while for us to admit this is clutter because the objects are so small in size. It's only when they build into a pile or they continually get in our way that we begin to admit the obvious: it's clutter just like most of everything else.

- **Finally, don't ignore the largest surface in your home**: the floor. It's so large that we rarely notice if there's clutter on it. It can easily get nudged away to the side and we forget that clutter is there at all, especially since it's at our feet. Don't allow yourself to neglect the floor in your home. Soon your floor will be hidden under clutter and you will struggle just to go from the kitchen to the bathroom. This can kill enthusiasm and productivity. Reserve the ground for the rug, your feet and the furniture. Remove all other objects!

**5. Use small units of organization** - Your home will benefit from an organization system developed for the efficient arrangement of stuff. These small organizational units will consist of items that serve a related purpose. These items should be kept together in a specific storage location such as drawers, containers or boxes. This will make it easier to find them. If you are in need of a pair of scissors, you won't have to go searching through the toolbox in the garage; instead you can look through the small organization box containing sewing tools. When you are looking for the blue flash drive containing your son's graduation photos, you won't have to launch a search party to find it under the bed. It will be there lying in the drawer under the computer table. Doesn't that sound like the kind of life you want to live?

Organizing your belongings into smaller units with similar functions helps you keep stock of what you own, what you need and what you should release. It's only when you gather all the duct tape you own into one place that you realize there are three other rolls that you completely forgot about. This technique will help you curb the accumulation of materials that can grow into a clutter if left unchecked.

Once you've gathered all these supplies into their various groups, it's time to throw away the excess. Five hammers, sevens pairs of scissors, ten cutlery sets, and all these for a family of four. Do you really need all of these items in your home? Cut down the number of your possessions until you arrive at a more reasonable number. Reclaim your space from all of this excess. Go through these collections and save only the favorites.

**6. Let in one and let another go** - Decluttering can turn out to be a very frustrating process for people who haven't learned to control the inflow of stuff into their lives. You might have done everything perfectly, from categorizing your stuff and put them into their appropriate containers to keeping all your surfaces clear, but you may still find there is a lack of progress. There's still clutter in some parts of the house. You might wonder why that is. Think of your home as a hole and you hold a shovel, digging out sand from the hole. You dig as hard as you can and exclaim with joy once you see your hole is bigger than ever, with more space than you could have ever imagined. Now picture someone else shoveling in more sand just minutes after you've finished. Soon the hole gets filled up again. This is what seems to happen when some of us declutter. We end up almost exactly where we began. We clear away excess but then find ourselves *still* with excess. It doesn't matter how much sand you remove if you end up filling it with more sand later.

To prevent this from happening, do one simple thing: whenever you buy something new, get rid of something old. For every new book that finds its way into your personal library, your least favorite will leave the library. It is as simple as that. If a brand new ceramic bowl finds a space in the kitchen shelf, an older one should be given away.

**7. Establish workable routines:** At this point, due to the growing excitement that comes with picturing a decluttered home, you might think you have gotten all the principles at your fingertips. Yes, we have been able to thoroughly examine some of them, but it doesn't stop there. Decluttering isn't a one-off activity where when we are done, we are done for life. Clutter is always waiting at your doorstep getting ready to invade again. You have to be on the constant lookout. It is just like a weed. You can cut it down as much as you want but until the root is addressed, it will always rear its ugly head again. The root of clutter is in your habits. What differentiates a minimalist from a non-minimalist are good habits. To succeed at minimalism, you must change the habits that govern your everyday life.

Vigilance is key. Live intentionally. Remember to always act as a gatekeeper and protect your home from excesses. Allow these principles to become second nature to you until you can no longer exist in the presence of the slightest clutter. Block unnecessary ads on your browser if you're materialistic and easily influenced by ads. Pay off debt and allow your mind to become more free. Cancel subscriptions that are no longer necessary for your business so your mail can stay organized.

Practice your decluttering process until you become nearly perfect. You may decide on a one-day-at-a-time approach. Dispose of one item each day. It won't take much effort or time. Just be consistent with it until you master it and it becomes part of you. One day you will discover that you have the drive to dispose of more than just one item. Once your donation or trash box is full, send it off to its specified destination.

Finally, set decluttering goals in your journal so that you know how much progress you are making. Tick off your goals as you achieve them as a form of self-encouragement and motivation. Don't forget to appreciate yourself for the efforts made once you hit a new milestone. Celebrate your resilience throughout the process and your mind will be fired up to do more. Just make sure you have fun with the process. See it as a game - a game that is capable of changing your life.

## Questions You Must Ask Yourself Before You Buy Anything

A lot of people in this modern world are only trying to make more money so they can buy more stuff. And some others are even trying to pay off the debt they accumulated the last time they splurged. Don't get tangled up in this way of life. It is a cycle that never ends. To ensure you prevent this from happening, ask yourself the following questions whenever you feel the urge to buy something:

1. **Am I financially equipped for this purchase?**

This is where it begins. If you don't have the money for the purchase, why are you considering it in the first place? Consider the debt this might put on you. And consider what you're giving up by buying this product. If you buy this now, it means you can't buy something else down the road. Will this lead to you skipping a meal or having to live without a more essential product?

2. **Do I need this or am I just buying it because it's on sale?**

Impulse purchases are one of the biggest killers of minimalism and one of the biggest magnets for clutter. A genuine need will come up again and again. If it doesn't, then you can do without the item that satisfies that urge. Make sure that all your purchases are planned and not just a spur of the moment decision. Don't just buy it as soon as you want it; give yourself time to assess your situation and budget completely. If you're buying it for a valid reason and it's a necessary purchase, you will know.

3. **Do I already own something similar to this or can it easily be rented?**
Before you run off to buy something new, check to confirm that you don't already own something similar to it at home. You'll find some items in your home can be repurposed. Instead of going out to get some new containers, why not use the older ones that can just be washed and reused? If you are in need of a power tool to carry out a project, you can easily rent or borrow one from a neighbor instead of buying a whole new tool that will likely only be used once every half-year. By renting or reusing, you are saving yourself a whole lot of money.

4. **If I don't buy a higher quality product, what's the likelihood I'll have to replace this?**
'Quality over quantity' should be one of your mantras. The quality of the product should be your major priority because if you end up with something substandard, you'll have to shell out money for another one very soon. Why not save yourself the stress and buy something that will last a whole lot longer? Ask yourself: "Is the quality worth the price?" Maybe you want to get a new set of upholstery and you notice that the stitches are already coming undone on one side. Before spending all your money, consider using it to get something more long-lasting. It is pure joy seeing an item you bought years ago still serving its purpose with little to no wear and tear.

## The 30-Day Wishlist Strategy

One way to tackle unnecessary purchases is by employing the 30 day wishlist strategy. The method here is simple: every time you feel the need to purchase something, write the name of that item on a list. This list can be anywhere: your phone, your journal, or even a note on the fridge. Each time you jot down an item, write down next to it what the date is. This will serve as a record of your spending urges and the day you felt each one. What you're going to do is wait at least 30 days before you consider buying this item. This will give you a lot of time to research the item and to see if you still want it after a lot of time has passed. For more expensive purchases, consider stretching 30 days to a longer period of time. If you decide you still want the item after 30 days or more, and you're sure you don't already own an item similar, then go ahead and buy it.

# CHAPTER FOUR - FREE YOURSELF FROM EMOTIONAL AND MENTAL CLUTTER

We handled various ways in which we can take care of physical clutter, but clutter does not end there. Clutter occurs in our mind too. When people complain about emotional instability or depression, it is simply because of emotional clutter. They have ignored the main focus of existence and have begun chasing the meaningless things in life - things that only clog the mind and lead nowhere.

The building blocks of the mind are thoughts. Once our thoughts have been managed, then mind clutter can be dealt with. These thoughts can be positive, negative or neutral and just like your home is cluttered with possessions, your mind can also become cluttered with thoughts. If they are positive thoughts, then you are on the safe side. But that is not usually the case. Unfortunately it is not as easy to deal with mental and emotional clutter as it is to deal with physical clutter. You can't just discard a thought and expect it to not return. It doesn't work that way.

Sometimes it seems like these thoughts have mechanisms and minds of their own, and they can sometimes control you. Constructive thinking is necessary to help out with problem-solving, analyses, decision making, and planning, but despite all of this, the mind can produce negativity out of nowhere. This forms an inner distraction from the physical world around you. Have you ever come across someone on the subway that went past their designated stop just because they were deep in their thoughts? That signifies a dangerous emotional clutter. They are gradually losing touch with the physical world. These negative thoughts mostly spring up as a result of assuming that the harder you think about your predicaments, the easier it will be for you to get out them. Of course, we know perfectly well that it is a flawed ideology, yet we hold on to it. Why? It is because these thoughts have already created a stronghold in the mind. Soon you discover that you have been caught up in a constant loop of regretful thinking about your past and anxiety for the future.

These thoughts become such an integral part of your mind that you begin to think that there is nothing that can be done about it. You can't just shut down your brain and have it stop processing some thoughts. Negative thoughts are like a virus on a computer. You can reboot the system and it's still there when you turn it back on. You can sleep, wake up again, and your thoughts will continue to bother you. You have to deal with them squarely before you ruin your week.

All of your thoughts might be unconscious, but you can manage them by practicing intentionality. You have far more control over your mind than you think. You just have to be willing to exercise that control. Once you've managed your emotional clutter, you will discover an immense amount of creativity and inspiration that awaits you, hidden under all of that clutter.

## Factors that Facilitate Mental Clutter

Before we set about trying to deal with mental and emotional clutter, it is necessary that we tackle the root problem. Where does all of this clutter emanate from?

- **Stress**

Stress can easily overwhelm you and overpower your motivation to live. Stress is associated with a variety of mental issues such as depression, anxiety and panic attacks. When combined with worries, negative thoughts and other concerns that burden our daily life, the problem only multiplies. Sleep becomes affected. Anger management issues may set in. Headaches and chest pains become the order of the day.

The stress can manifest itself in a variety of ways, for example, in a toxic work environment, domestic violence at home, or even a problematic child. Things turn out to be so complicated and intense that your mind loses the ability to control itself.

- **An Excess of Material Objects**

We handled this in a preceding chapter. Once your life and home become too clogged and cluttered with stuff, your mind begins to suffer. In the modern age, we are so eager to fill up our homes with useless possessions that have no true value and can be done without. All of this stuff contributes to time consumption, becomes a financial drain and induces anxiety.

People who are propelled to live their lives based on the quantity of physical possessions they own are always on the competitive side. Nothing is ever enough for them. They will always want to keep up with the latest trends no matter what it will cost them financially or emotionally. Decluttering your life of these things will ultimately help to curb the effects of negative thinking and anxiety.

- **A Litany of Choices**

Too much choice and variety can subtly lead to depression and anxiety. At first it might seem like the perfect life, to have a load of choices to decide from, but upon a closer analysis you will discover the unadmirable quality of it. What should be a decision that can be made in mere seconds will lead to days of agonizing contemplation. A litany of choices is brain-draining and stressful.

## Must-Know Practices to Help You Deal with Mental Clutter

1. **Meditation**

Certain misconceptions may deter you from practicing meditation. Truth is, you don't have to be a Buddhist monk, a psychic, or even a certified witch to practice meditation. Don't get scared by the stories you hear about cave dwellers who meditate for months at a time. There are levels of meditation, and at this point, we are only going to tackle the basic levels of it. Meditation does not belong to people of a certain religious faith or spiritual inclination.

The only thing is that meditation and the reason for performing it vary from one meditator to another. For this chapter, meditation will be considered a tool to help you control your mind and your thoughts. You can practice meditation anywhere you feel like it. You don't necessarily need a quiet environment, but you must be able to achieve that quietness on the inside. That way, it will be easier for you to sort through your thoughts and pick out those that should be discarded. The benefits of practicing meditation are numerous, both for your physical wellbeing and also for the emotional side of your life.

The main point is to practice meditation consistently. You cannot reap its full benefits without constant practice. Commit to practicing meditation at a scheduled time every single day. That way, you will improve your ability to control your mind mechanisms and put them in check.

Meditation doesn't have to take long. All you have to do is to find a spot and sit still. Set out a specific time every day that you will carry out your meditation and stick to it. Don't choose an overly comfortable position so that you don't fall asleep while meditating. Turn off every digital device that's capable of producing noise or any distractions. Try and time yourself, so you know when you have done enough. For beginners, five minutes is enough time to meditate effectively.

Make sure you are ready for the process, and nothing else will distract you. For the next five minutes, focus on your breathing. Count the number of breaths you take in and out of your body. Notice how the air leaves you and returns into your nostrils. Observe the rise and fall of your chest region. Allow your breath to flow naturally; don't try to control them. This will help you build focus. At first, you might encounter problems keeping focus but try and return your attention to your breathing each time.

Close your eyes to avoid visual distractions. The goal of meditation is to shut thoughts out of your mind. By focusing on the breath, you are taking attention away from anything that causes you stress. Wave off the negative and store the positives so you can ruminate on them when the time finally arrives.

2. **Deal with the negative thoughts**

A lot of people go through life everyday with negative thoughts floating across the surface of their minds. They have become victims of a mental flood and if care is not taken, they may drown. The negative voices in their heads speak louder and louder until they can't even hear themselves. This form of negativity can be given strength and a stronghold in the mind if it is not challenged at the initial stage.

The first step is to notice these thoughts before they get out of control. Notice the pattern with which they operate in your mind. You can employ these strategies to help you out:

a. **Be Watchful**

You don't always need to have an emotional reaction to all your thoughts. Sometimes you should take yourself out of the scene and become a spectator. Observe what is going on in your mind. Notice how your thoughts interact with one another. Don't judge any of these thoughts negatively or positively. Just sit back and observe.

b. **See your thoughts for what they really are**

Although they are powerful enough to alter whole facets of your life, understand these are thoughts and nothing more. They are not real for the time being, but they have the capability to become real if you don't manage them.

c. **Put up a roadblock**

You own your mind, right? They you should be able to determine what comes in, what stays and what goes out. Whenever you catch yourself in a mental state that makes you uncomfortable, learn to scold yourself and stop the reaction. You can be vocal about your refusal to think those thoughts. Say, "I refuse to be caught by negative thoughts in this web of distractions." Build walls around your mind, strongholds that will serve to protect you whenever the time arrives.

d. **Know the causes**

Every negative thought in your mind is caused or triggered by a certain factor. It could be a person, another thought, a situation or even a physical state. The next time you find yourself wallowing in these thoughts, take the time to find out what triggered the thoughts. Chances are that they will be lying there waiting to be discovered and dealt with.

Write down the major triggers that come to your mind. Brood over them for a while and see if you can find any solutions to them. If it's something that you can solve by yourself, such as the reconciliation of a wrecked relationship or working on your own flaws, then go ahead and deal with these thoughts. If you discover that you have no power over the situation at hand such as an inability to travel because of bad weather or a miscarriage, make up your mind to be happy regardless. You caused none of it so there is no need to feel bad about it.

### f. Occupy your mind

Each day you wake, you wake up with a clear mind, a tabula rasa. If you leave it empty, the mind has a way of creating something to do for its own self. Ever noticed how your mind is never empty, how at every point in time you are always ruminating and considering an issue? The mind is only inactive when you are asleep, and that is if it doesn't get overwhelmed by dreams. So once you wake up, give your mind something creative to do. Focus your brainpower on important projects that will help fulfill a long term goal. Give yourself something positive to worry about, like how you can get a PhD. If you find yourself stuck in traffic, pick up a book, and read or search for an insightful TED talk and listen to it.

### 3. Subdue your mind under your control

You are the boss here. Your mind belongs to you, and you should never give up control. Never let it run through the thoughts you don't want to process. Get your mind under control so that each time, you are pleased by the outcome it produces. You can achieve this by practicing the following:

a. **Identifying the wrong thoughts and replacing them**: The wrong thoughts are easy to identify; they can be spotted from miles away. Once your mind begins to process them, you notice a certain kind of weight hovering over you. And they are mostly exaggerated. Funny enough, the wrong thoughts are very pleasing to hold. You just lost your job at 50, and you begin to think, "I am a total failure. Can anything good come out of me?" You know you should not be thinking that way, but it seems very comfortable to dwell in that state of mind. Why? Well, no one thinks positive thoughts after a bad experience. If you examine that thought closely and truthfully, you will discover that it is not entirely true. Somebody somewhere admires you for who you are irrespective of your current financial state.

Instead of keeping yourself in that state, why not challenge your negative thoughts with positive ones? Reassure yourself that you are not a failure or a loser. Thinking you are one will not automatically make you a success. How many times have you gone into a job interview and one of the interviewers says, "Well, it seems you have always thought of yourself as a failure. We are going to give you the job to help you stop seeing yourself that way." It doesn't happen. In fact, people who breed negative thoughts are always repulsive to others. For every person who has given a negative comment about you or your work, there are about ten more making positive remarks. So why are you allowing that one comment to spoil your mood and corrupt your other thoughts?

b. **Accept the situation but don't get comfortable with it**

What do you do when the negative thoughts swirling around your mind are true? How will you be able to cope with the situation triggering these negative thoughts? It is hard to challenge negative thoughts with positivity when the truth is staring right at you. You just lost your home and all of your property to fire. Your grades are going down the drain and at this rate you are probably not going to graduate.

These are negative thoughts about situations that cannot be eliminated, but you can reduce the effect that they have on your mind by accepting the situation at hand, not the thoughts. It happened, and there is nothing you can do about the past, but you can change the future. Don't begin to nurture guilt about your carelessness, or go on about how things could have been better. You are only making your head foggier and clogging up your emotions. At this point, your best bet for a solution is to find peace of mind.

Accepting the situation will help you identify ways to improve or solve the problem at hand. There is always a brighter side, no matter how dim it may be, and it can only be identified with a clear mind.

c. **Take necessary actions**

Worrying and strategizing are two different things. Worrying is easier but its results can be bad for you. Strategy requires mental energy that most of us are not willing to sacrifice. The truth is that worry gets you nowhere; it is better you employ strategy. The downside of worry is that you expend so much energy producing negative thoughts and you never come up with a solution. All that energy you spent worrying could have been put towards strategizing, and perhaps your problem would be fixed by now.

**Identify Your Core Values**

A major challenge that people of this age face is the inability to identify what is truly important to their existence. In our world today, there are so many distractions that take away from what we need. We are bombarded by marketing and meaningless messages, and we rarely go inward, connecting to our inner voice. These things can become such an overload that the process of prioritizing our values becomes a major task. This makes it very necessary to reevaluate what is most important to us with each passing day. Rise over all of the societal noise by defining your core values.

Identifying your core values is one sure way to help you combat clutter, both physically and mentally. These principles will help you spend time, energy, and money doing the things that help you in the long run. The presence of core values enables you to keep focus. It is easier to spot distractions. A lot of the highest achievers of our age are people who have identified their core values. Once, during an interview, Steve Jobs stated that he kept his wardrobe streamlined to simple black turtlenecks, blue jeans, and New Balance sneakers. Why? So that his wardrobe decisions didn't take up a lot of brainpower and he could focus on what really matters. That reply reflects the mindset of someone who has identified his core values. Try to picture how organized and minimalistic his closet probably looked.

## How to Identify Your Core Values

Core values are not selected; they are discovered or revealed. It is easy to say that physical fitness is one of your core values, but when was the last time you actually exercised?

Deciding on your core values can be a daunting task, but what you find out about yourself will help you. In case you are unfamiliar with the core values terrain, let's go through some lists and identify some values that appeal to you. From there, you can streamline them into your perfect options. These can help you identify your core values:

**a.      Your peak experiences**
What do you consider a very important moment in your life? What makes that moment standout for you? What happened to you in that very moment? What values came into play to make this moment a very important one?

**b.      Suppressed values**
This is the opposite of the first one. Here, consider the values that cruised through you when you were the most angry and irritated. What got you angry during those moments? Those are your suppressed values. They never seem to rear their heads but they are there as relevant as ever.

**c.      Brainstorming**

Brainstorming involves more of a general search. You ask yourself questions that only you can answer. Pick a pen and a jotter and provide answers to these questions:
- What values in others attracts me the most?
- What drives me the most in life?
- What do I admire most about myself?
- What's one virtue I never want to lose?

While answering these questions, you will certainly run into moments of clarity and understanding and you will find your core values waiting on the other side of reflection.

**d.   Ask the people around you**

Sometimes people around you notice things you might ignore about yourself. For example, someone who is neat or organized might not necessarily understand how neat or organized he or she is until people point it out and commend them for it. It is just like using a particular cologne brand for years. Soon the fragrance blends in naturally with your nose and your olfactory nerves fail to interpret the smell because they have been doing so for a long time. Until the day someone points it out to you, you might never understand how much it has become a part of you.

Your core values are like this. People see your values before you even notice them, so their opinions can be very necessary for helping you identify these values. Look for the smart and observant people around you and ask them to define you and what they think you stand for. You will be amazed by the responses you receive. There is no way that you won't be able to identify your core values after following these steps.

# Everything You Need to Know About Decluttering Your Relationships

You need people in your life, but they can sometimes be great hindrances. Once your relationships begin to falter, an unbalance sets in and soon, you're overcome by distress. The painful question, "Who can I trust?" begins to haunt you.

A popular saying goes, "We disagree to agree." Misunderstandings and reconciliations are some of the blocks that build and strengthen a relationship. But when these interactions constantly leave you worn out and emotionally drained, then it's high time you either try to mend broken bridges or remove the other party from your life.

You will never understand the importance of having healthy relationships until you try to imagine a life without any form of anxiety relating to the people in it. The most productive people are those who have created a perfect balance in every relationship, be it their relationship with their spouse, children, bosses or even the person beside them on the train.

Relationship clutter can build up in a variety of ways such as minor-major arguments, malice keeping, hatred, envy, jealousy, and the likes. Once they gain enough ground, they clog up your mind. Think back to the last time you felt annoyed by your best friend, or when you envied someone so much that you could taste the gall in your own throat. Think back and consider how heavy your heart felt in those moments. Then try to remember the feeling you had when there was an embrace of reconciliation. Can you feel how light your heart was in that moment and the deep breaths you took afterward? That's the beauty of a decluttered mind. Space is instantly created for something else, something worthwhile.

It is not just about having relationships but having quality relationships. Here's another saying: "It is better to make one true friend in a thousand years than to make one thousand fake acquaintances in one year." The beauty of relationships is not in quantity but in quality. The ingredients that make up a great friendship will include:

- Shared Interests
- Mutual respect and trust
- Understanding and acceptance

- Openness and honesty
- Healthy conflict resolution

Creating relationships is necessary to your existence and this is why it is essential to take your time choosing the relationships you should invest in. The primary reason why the loss of a relationship hurts so much is because of our emotional investment.

To begin with, work on your relationships. Start with yourself. They say, "If you want to change the world, start with yourself." If you want to change your relationships, you should start with yourself. It might be so obvious and glaring that the other person in the relationship needs to make a change too, but ignore that fact and start with your own change. It will help you heal and do away with all the clutter. After all, you can't change others except if they agree to change themselves or be changed. These strategies will help you build healthier relationships:

### 1. INVEST YOURSELF (YOUR TIME AND PRESENCE)

Once I saw someone post a picture of a friend and caption it, "Thank you for being there. Happy Birthday." It was the first time I had seen such a short message used on a birthday post, but it was very profound. That word 'there' meant so much to the person who had posted the picture. But what exactly did he or she mean by 'there'?

'There' signifies presence and time. That friend was available when he was most needed. Those kinds of friends are hard to ignore or forget. They make themselves available during the darkest times of our lives. They are present when it matters. How present are you in your relationships? How much of yourself have you invested? Here is how to invest yourself into a relationship:
  1. Pay Attention

How do you feel when someone isn't paying any attention to something important you are saying? How does it feel when you know they aren't listening to something that means a lot to you? It is disheartening at best, and the chances that you will ever want to share a conversation with them are very slim. The truth, as bitter as it may sound, is that you have probably done it too, intentionally or unintentionally.

This mostly happens because of the numerous distractions in the mind that tend to monopolize your attention. This causes you to focus more on the crowd in your mind than on the person talking to you. Still, that is no excuse. Paying attention is the willingness to step out of all those distractions and listen, not just hear. Absorb the speaker and their words so that he or she will feel safe and comfortable talking to you. Make it all about the other person and what they are saying. Make each gesture count and try not to look distracted. These tips will help:

- Allow the speaker to dominate the conversation until they ask for your opinion
- Avoid unnecessary interruptions, except if you have something really important to say.
- Hear the full story before jumping to conclusions.
- Keep your gestures and facial expressions as neutral as possible.

Paying attention might look one-sided, like the speaker is the only one who benefits during the interaction, but learning to listen and shut out the noise in your mind is a huge benefit to you. In fact, it is one way of helping you declutter your mind and be more present.

a. Positive speaking and encouragement

Language matters in every conversation. Don't rush to spill the contents of your mind. First, probe them and anticipate a reaction before you release them. Negative comments are products of negative thoughts and can be damaging to a relationship.

Pay close attention to the things you say during a conversation. It might not seem to matter, but the other person may feel differently.

Recognize that each word is powerful and can create a different effect to what was intended. Don't say, "But you should have known better, especially with all of your education." Say, "It was a learning moment for you, and I am happy you learned the lesson." Don't say, "You acted so stupidly." Say, "I don't think that was the right thing to do at that moment." Speak with love and compassion.

Mastering the art of compassionate communication will make others want to talk and relate to you. Resist the temptation to be judgmental about other people's actions. Put yourself in their shoes and try to understand why they act the way they do. When you master the art of being kind in all forms, the people around you will mirror the same actions, and your relationships will blossom further. Of course, you already have an idea of how good that will be for your emotions. You will find peace in your inner world, and it will reflect into the world around you.

    b. Find reasons to love

No matter how bad a person is, there is always one reason to love them. Find that reason and cling to it. Of course, we have been told to love people unconditionally, but human nature makes that hard to do. Sometimes it is best to find reasons to love them even when it seems like they should not be loved. Reducing the negative thoughts you have about people in your life can significantly improve your relationship with them.

Studies have shown that when we think positively about others, it leads to increased contentment in life, kindness towards others in general, hope and enthusiasm to build better relationships. How you decide to practice the art of positive thinking is up to you. You can do it by meditating on their good characters, or you can do it by saying positive things about them. The point of this practice is to transform your mind and declutter your emotions.

    c. Eliminate comparison

Comparison is a prison that many people are locked in. Comparing yourself to others is one sure way to hold you back from any form of progress. Comparisons are fertile ground for breeding negative thoughts. "Am I good enough?" "Do I have what it takes to be admired like he or she is?" "Will I ever be that attractive?"

These thoughts can build up and get out of control until low self-esteem takes control of your thoughts. Most times, constant comparison can also lead to mild hatred for the person you are comparing yourself to. There is a high possibility of you viewing them as the reason for your unhappiness, even when this is an entirely unfair accusation. And there is no way you can have a healthy relationship with someone whom you feel this way about. Each time you see them, something shifts inside of you. Your mind begins to act abnormally.

You are on your own journey in life, and only you can understand your struggles. This is why we handled the issue of core values. A person who has discovered his or her true core values cannot be affected by comparisons to others because they already have a focus. Other people's journeys don't affect them.

Don't get me wrong, from time to time comparisons can take a positive turn, and that is something you should be on the lookout for. Use comparisons to motivate yourself and work harder to become a better person. Comparisons can help you identify places in your life that need to be worked on and improved. But when you begin to notice its excesses, and it takes a negative turn, turn it down a little. The mental effort involved in comparisons can drain you. Never allow it to grow out of your control. These tips can help you combat comparison:

☐ Accept Yourself

You are perfect the way you are, not because you are actually perfect but because you choose to believe that you are perfect. You can't change anything about yourself unless you have hundreds of dollars stashed up somewhere to spend on plastic surgery. Good luck with that and I only pray that you don't come out looking more messed up than before.

Instead of battling to change who you are, you can do a quick job of accepting yourself. No amount of comparison or worry will change who you are. Most people are more receptive to people who have accepted themselves for who they are. Self-acceptance is self-liberation and self-empowerment.

- Improve what needs to be improved

Change the things about yourself that can be changed. Are you insecure about your appearance? Work on your wardrobe or your hairstyle. Have you noticed that more people are attracted to someone who smiles? Then try to have more gentle facial expressions. Sometimes, no matter how much you try, you might never be able to match up to the people you admire and compare yourself to. Don't sweat it. Simply find something that makes you exceptional and work on it. Your core values and life priorities should be the main factor in helping you define your life. Sometimes we are attracted to qualities in others that we don't need. She has longer legs. So what, are you trying to become a long jumper? You are a writer, so the longer legs shouldn't matter to you. Focus on your strengths, the things that make you unique. Somebody out there that you don't even know yet thinks you are awesome because of them.

- Practice Gratitude

I talked about this in chapter three, but it still remains an important tip. You can forget to feel gratitude when you become too focused on what another person has. You begin to ignore the beautiful things that life has brought your way, simply because you are missing out on some other little things.

Gratitude is about committing to the bright side. It's a commitment to creating joy even when it feels like there's none at all. There are good things in your life and they should never be ignored. Focus on them for at least three to five minutes every day before going to bed or after waking up. I advise making gratitude part of your morning routine since it's a great way to start your day, but if you have busy mornings, a nightly gratitude routine works just fine as well. Take a moment to think about how blessed you are. It can be surprisingly liberating.

## 2. RELEASE YOURSELF FROM YOUR PAST

Carrying the burdens of the past is one way to hold yourself back from seeing the light in your relationships and life, in general. You may have been in some toxic relationships before now, but there is a time to let these lingering feelings go. It is natural for the mind to keep replaying scenarios and hurt over and over. However, this process should not take over any part of our lives. Having these memories return over and over can create wells of anger, guilt, and shame. These thoughts keep you stuck to the past, drain the positivity in the present, and rob your future. You not only clutter your emotions; you also imprison your mind and hinder its productivity.

It is hard to let go of pain from the past, but it can still be done. A lot of people have succeeded in doing it. You can, too. The benefits of letting go are enormous. Not only will you have more positivity because you create positivity, but you will likely also see more positive things come into your life. Why? Because we are a magnet for our life circumstances. Exude positivity, and you'll attract positivity. So, step one, let go of your past. Try the following tips:

### a. Make Resolutions and Stick to Them

People get a strange amount of comfort from wallowing in pain, but we should always resist this urge. It gets nothing solved. Sometimes the people you feel have hurt you have no idea that they ever did that. Take action and find ways to resolve any issue that you feel needs to be resolved. Take out time to communicate with the person and clear the air. No matter how fresh the hurt is, you should try to talk things out instead of bearing a useless burden and clogging your mind.

Don't go into the reconciliation process with a bitter heart. That will only make the dialogue process difficult. Healthy communication is paramount for you to reach a sensible solution; if not, your discussion may be hostile. Most of the process will involve listening to the other party's grievances and understanding how you hurt them. There will be apologies and a call to forgiveness, then a final resolution.

Keep an open mind while discussing and resolving issues. When you dwell on your hurt, your perspective begins to feel like the only true angle, but this is not true at all. Be flexible and see things from another person's perspective. Put yourself in other people's shoes. Ask yourself questions, such as:

- What exactly made this person get angry and say what he or she said?
- What actions or words of yours were misinterpreted and taken the wrong way?
- Is there a possibility you've interpreted the situation in the wrong way?

Be flexible enough to challenge your own point of view. Rigidity does not help you in your empathy, it only clings to its own beliefs, even when they are incorrect and unhelpful. Compromise your stance for the sake of your friendships.

### b. Forgiveness

They might never ask for forgiveness, but forgive anyway. This is for your sake as well, not just the other person's. The more people you vow not to forgive, the more files and tabs are open in the browser of your mind. Imagine how slow your computer would be, if it was invested in so many needless things as your mind. It is time to close some tabs! Clinging to all that trash only makes you suffer. Free yourself now!

Forgiveness doesn't mean you're playing the fool and allowing someone to come into your life and hurt you again. Forgiveness is letting go of all resentment and anger so you are no longer holding onto poison. Forgiveness is hard to give when the other party still hasn't taken responsibility for their actions. Understand that they are on a lower level of understanding and there is no need to stoop so low or act on their level.

# CHAPTER FIVE – THE SECRETS OF FINANCIAL MINIMALISM

As new as it may sound to you, financial minimalism is a real concept, and it comes with real benefits. Some of us might have even practiced it without knowing that we were being financially minimalistic. While most of us focus on decluttering our homes and our physical environment, minimalism can also be applied to financial health. All the times you restrained yourself from spending extravagantly, that was financial minimalism. Enrolling in a cashless economy is financial minimalism.

Budgeting, which is a major aspect of financial minimalism, will give more clarity on your spending and help you with your financial priorities. Financial minimalism is not about spending less money, but about only spending money when you need to. It advocates against spending whenever you feel like it. Financial minimalism is about spending intentionally, keeping control of every penny, and not letting any amount slip through your fingers.

## How Minimalism Can Help You Financially

1. Financial minimalism helps you to minimize your spending

With financial minimalism, you're only going to purchase the items or services that mean the most to you. Once you have set your purchasing priorities straight, you will naturally have more control over your spending habits. The way you spend money changes when you are focused on acquiring specific items and not just living on a spur-of-the-moment basis. When you spend more intentionally, you naturally begin to save more money.

2. Less excess in your home

Once you are able to control your spending, you automatically control the accumulation of excess in your life. Financial minimalism helps you keep track of the things you already own so you don't continue to buy the same thing, creating clutter. You'll see the results of your intentional spending in the space you live in. Over time, less clutter will form and you'll manage your space far more easily.

3. Gives you more focus for your financial goals

Financial minimalism helps you understand the importance of a financial budget. You spend with a plan, with an aim. Budgeting helps to streamline your spending based on your current needs. It will also help you to identify areas where you have to change the way you handle money. With less money coming out of your accounts, it's much easier to keep your financial goals in sight.

4. Freedom from debt

A good way to simplify your financial life is to get out of debt. In fact, it's difficult to get control over your finances if you still have a lot of debt. Debt can have the same effect on your finances as negative thinking does on your mind. With financial minimalism, it will be easy for you to pinpoint the factors that lead to debt accumulation and tackle them. And on top of this, you will be in a much better position to pay off debt now that you're saving more money due to your new minimalist lifestyle.

5. Giving becomes easier for you

When you have more financial security, you're able to give more without restriction. You're spending less on yourself, so you can give to others when they need it. When you practice financial minimalism, it is easier for you to recognize what and how much of it you can give. While budgeting for the month, you can cut down on some expenses and donate the extra money instead. That way you keep track of your money and know that nothing was wasted.

Minimalist Tips to Help You Achieve Financial Freedom

1. **Identify your financial values**

You must know the things that are important to you when it comes to money. It will be difficult for you to gain control over your finances if you haven't understood your values yet. Have a clear picture of the money habits in your life that needs to be eliminated. Pick out those that need to be adopted and work on assimilating them into your habits. Discover what your financial values are and start streamlining your budget to suit them. Some practices that you can adopt are:

- Never living above your means
- Eliminating the propensity to borrow
- Sticking to a budget
- Having an emergency fund

With these new practices in your life, it will be easier for you to cut out the non-essentials among your spending. Your financial goals will be reached with less stress and life becomes even simpler.

2. **Have an emergency fund**

Having an emergency fund is always a lifesaver. The amount you deposit into it will depend on how much you earn, and no matter how small your income is, make sure that a percentage of it goes into the emergency fund. Transfer money into your emergency fund and then carry on with the rest of the month. Don't think of it as another source of money for whenever you want to spend. As its name suggests, it is reserved for emergencies. You have to practice thorough discipline if you want to be successful with it. Whenever you have to take from it, make sure you add more money into it later to maintain a reasonable balance.

3. **Employ digital help**

There are many fantastic apps in the app store that will help you pay your bills automatically without causing you any stress. All you need is to input your payment method, the scheduled time for the payment, and the amount to be paid. A few days before the payment is to be made, you will be alerted about the incoming deductions. Some of these apps will also help you keep track of how much you spent on a particular service over a period of time. By making full use of these apps, you never have to worry about making a payment on time (and potentially creating debt!), and you save a little bit of time every month.

4. **Develop a budgeting system that works and stick to it**

Do you want to spend less than you make? Then the solution is simple: you need a budget. Budgeting helps you to manage expenses and never spend more than you can afford. Regardless of how much you make, the money that leaves your hands every month should never be more than what comes in; if it is, you stand a risk of running into more debt. It sounds like something everyone should be able to do easily, but this isn't the case at all.

Group your expenses into categories to help you keep track of how much you spend on each category. Keep the categories as consolidated as possible, so the list doesn't grow too long. Common categories include utilities, phone bills, transportation, rent, food, and miscellaneous. The contents of the list will differ from person to person due to various reasons, but they should share streamlined equality. Brainstorm and estimate how much you spend for each category per month and use that to create your final budget.

It is one thing to have a budget; it is another thing to stick to it. Don't create a budget for the sake of creating a budget. Resist the urge to sit back and suddenly feel that everything is going to be okay. Your work is not done! Discipline should bind you to your budget. Temptations will arise and try to surface your old habits, so prepare yourself for this. Keep your focus on your core financial values, and you will always come out successful.

5. **Minimize debt**

## Minimalism & Decluttering

Simply put, "Debt is money stolen from your future savings." And who said time travel wasn't a thing, when people are stealing from their future selves every day. You can always find the discipline to prevent yourself from falling into debt, no matter how tight the situation may seem. Seek out other options. Shift your mentality towards owning things that you can afford at the present moment, instead of buying things on credit and insisting you'll get your act together later. The peace of mind that comes from having no debt is far more rewarding than the fleeting high your spur-of-the-moment purchase gave you.

### 6. Find the best deals

Whenever you need to purchase something, take your time to research and find the best deals around. It may take a little bit of time, but the end result is worth it. You'll still get the exact same thing, but you'll be spending less money. Don't be so hasty to spend your hard-earned dollars just because you can afford it. Saving some money by finding the best deal will leave you with more money after the transaction. You can put this towards your savings or purchase something else that you need. You'll be amazed by the number of discounts offered. You just have to find them. And remember, although you should go for the best deal, make sure it is still for a high or above-average quality product.

### 7. Get rid of distractions

Think deeply and try to identify all the potential distractions from your financially minimalist life. What are the temptations that push you to buy things that you do not need? If you're subscribed to a particular store that always sends you compelling articles that lead you to buy their products, then unsubscribe. Unfollow social media influencers that are constantly tempting you into buying new products you don't need. If there is something or someone in your life, making you feel like your life is incomplete, remove that trigger. You won't be sorry and you won't be lesser for it. With these distractions out of the way, you can finally focus all your attention on doing right by your finances and your life.

# CHAPTER SIX - ADVANCED HOME DECLUTTERING

Now it's time for you to put all your new decluttering skills to work. In this chapter, we will be going through the various rooms in the house. I will be providing you with some tips on how to get rid of the excess in these rooms and defeat clutter instantly. Start from the room that feels most comfortable to you or the room with the most clutter. It is your call. Just make sure you actually begin the process and keep up with it. You don't have to follow the exact order I am going to detail here. At this point, the decluttering principles we studied in chapter three will be very important. Use them to guide you through the decluttering process of each room. The tips in this chapter will only be the basics.

## A Room-by-Room Decluttering Guide

### 1. LIVING ROOM

First, visualize your living room as you want it. Identify the furniture you want to keep and the ones that you will leave. Figure out all the things that should be on the shelves and the surface spaces.

Next, begin to ditch all of those things that will hinder your living room from being the perfect living room. Purging unnecessary items one day at a time will make a dramatic impact and transform your sitting-room within days. Consider the values that each item brings into the general sitting-room ambiance. Ask yourself questions about each item. Do the decorative objects really provide the joy and satisfaction that have been attributed to their presence? Have they become too old and outdated? Are they a little worn? And most importantly, do you even like them or are they gifts you just feel you *have to* like?

Send everything into its space. Figure out the areas to store your DVDs, games, and computer. Make sure that every other object in the sitting-room is kept in their appropriate area. All surfaces should remain clear, and stray objects should not be found on surfaces that do not belong to them. The surfaces in question include coffee tables, side tables, and desks. The sitting room floor should be kept tidy too.

Set a limit for the number of furniture and decorative materials that will exist in the sitting-room at any given time. Limit the things collected into the sitting-room. Display fewer items so that attention doesn't get divided and clutter doesn't begin to form again. This is the space in which you will be receiving guests, so stay aware of the impression your sitting-room is leaving on people who visit you.

## 2. **BEDROOM**

The bedroom is one of the most cluttered parts of the house. Since it's one of the more private rooms in the house, we think that we can do anything here and it won't matter. It does matter. Maybe not to your guests, but it is affecting your ability to rest in this room.

Before you begin to declutter, take a moment to picture what you want your bedroom to look like after the decluttering process. What kind of room do you envision? Begin to remove all the things creating clutter.

You should select items to keep, donate or trash. You will come across items that should be taken out of the room to another room where they will serve more important purposes. Sort them into their own pile and take them out later, to be arranged in their new home.

Dividing the bedroom into zones is quite easy. There will be a space for sleeping, dressing, and, for some, working. Sort the things in the room into their various spaces and organize them neatly. Keep the things you will need most often very close to you, somewhere on your bedside table.

Deal with surfaces and plan out the items that should be found on them every day. The bed is the most important surface in the room, and it is necessary for your wellbeing. It should always be kept as clear, clean, and organized as possible. Eliminate all clutter that is forming on your bed. You should also organize your wardrobe so it will be easier to handle your clothes and prevent them from finding their way onto the bed.

3. **KITCHEN**

The kitchen is the powerhouse of the home. If it is in disarray, everybody in the home feels it. There will be missing cutlery, broken ceramics, wafts of dust underneath the cabinets and pests in every corner. Since perishables and food are kept in this room, you must keep this space clean. Otherwise, you may start to attract unwelcome little guests, in the form of rodents or cockroaches. Due to its significance, the kitchen is filled with a lot of appliances and other tools. Once the objects in this room build into a clutter, the functionality of this space becomes undermined.

The beauty of every kitchen is in its spaciousness and the availability of clear countertops. That is what makes it desirable to cook here. Think about how lovely it will be to have your cabinets and shelves organized in the most welcoming way.

The first thing to do is empty every single cabinet or shelf in the kitchen. Even if you are sure that you will be returning an item back to this space, remove it still. You might not know how much space it is taking up just by being in that spot. Plus, removing everything provides the opportunity to clean the cabinet.

Sort through the items and find those that should be kept, donated, or trashed. When was the last time you used a particular appliance? Is it even working still? With each item you pick, ask yourself these important questions that will help you reach a conclusion about the future of each item.

If you have never categorized the items in your kitchen, you should do that now. Break them into groups such as baking items, cutting tools, everyday appliances, and mugs. Find all excess and drop them into the donation box.

## Tips for Getting Rid of Sentimental Clutter

Some sentimental objects are worth keeping. Like a deceased relative's fur coat or a prized antique, but let's face it, there are some sentimental things that need to go. Do you really need your ex-boyfriend's old guitar picks? Or your mother's (no matter how deceased she may be) incredibly ugly old mugs? Probably not. Even if you know you don't want them or need them, they can still be hard to get rid of. Keep these tips in mind:

- **Eliminate all guilt**

Sometimes we don't throw away sentimental objects because we feel guilty. Think about where this guilt stems from. Is the object in question something that once belonged to an old relative? Do you feel bad because it's like you're throwing away a piece of them? Nip this thinking in the bud. People are not their possessions. Chances are you have something else from them that is far more useful and that doesn't create as much clutter. You are not harming anyone here, so don't feel guilty.

- **Focus on a different aspect of the memory**

Another reason why we keep sentimental things is because they are attached to a certain memory. This makes total sense. Luckily for you, you don't have to throw away the memory if you throw away the object. If you're throwing away an item connected to a memory, consider writing a journal entry about the memory instead. Immortalize it that way. Or look at old pictures of this memory. Let's say you're holding onto your mother's ugly mugs because she used to drink her favorite coffee out of them. Well, hold on a sec, you also live in the house where your mother used to drink her favorite coffee out of her ugly mugs. See the kitchen as the connection to this memory instead.

- **Give it to someone else**

If you know someone else who might want this item, consider giving it to them. This way, you don't have to see the object in the garbage. Someone out there still has it and still appreciates it. And if the object is something that belongs to someone else in the first place (like an ex-boyfriend), then give it back already! There's no use holding on.

## The Best Way to Decorate and Design a Minimalist Home

When decorating your minimalist home, you should keep three important factors in mind:

a. Quality
b. Spaciousness
c. Clear surfaces

These factors are more important than the subjective beauty of your decorative items. By keeping these factors in mind, almost any decorative item can look appealing. Use these tips to get started:

**1. Go for neutral colours**

Riots of color can sometimes appear as clutter. Try to keep your color combinations as simple and neutral as possible. Go for colors that inspire a feeling of calmness, whatever that means to you. It may not be the same color for everyone, but it's rarely bright or neon color. It doesn't mean that you cannot experiment with colors and get creative; it just means you should first study the colors you want, think about how those colors affect you and find out if they work well together. Ask yourself if the combination is easy on the eyes. Remember, this is your private, resting space. It's absolutely vital that you can relax here.

**2. Quality over quantity**

You should consider each piece carefully before you let it into your home. Work with few objects while decorating your home, but make sure that every single object is of a reasonable or high quality. Your goal is to create a comfortable space that anyone would be comfortable in. Choose well-made designs that are built to last. Since you will be using these objects a lot, it is important that they will survive more than a few uses.

### 3. Bring in nature

Florals and greenery will add a beautiful touch of nature to your sitting-room and kitchen. The colors from flowers or other plants will also add to the overall color scheme of your home. Keep this in mind when you are choosing your natural pieces. What's wonderful about plants is they bring in so much beauty and they last as long as you are able to take care of them. Hopefully, that is a long time! Be good to your plants.

### 4. Interesting accessories

The accessories in a room can change the entire look of the room. An accessory in this regard is anything that is added to a room to give it an aesthetic value. Throw in one or two well-selected accessories or decorations such as wall art, mirrors, candles, picture frames and rugs. Work with variety but try to maintain balance even as you work this into your space.

### 5. Keep it simple

The beauty of minimalism is in its simplicity. Adopt the 'less is more' approach to your interior décor. Continue to keep space in mind as you work. Your space doesn't have to be boring. In fact, minimalist decorations when done well can be far more beautiful than hordes of decorations staring at you from every corner. Just take it one step at a time and make sure to be fully committed to minimalist aesthetics.

# CHAPTER SEVEN - DIGITAL DECLUTTERING

Since the world went digital, our lives have become more comfortable, we have become more productive, and information dissemination is now faster. But there is a downside: we have also become obsessed with electronics and digital devices. The devotion we show these little gadgets has reached an alarming stage. Things that were produced for us to control have now gradually become our masters.

Here is a quick picture: hours on social media, hundreds of unread emails in our inboxes, a desktop littered with folders and files, storage devices filled with hundreds or even thousands of photos, music, and videos. It is overwhelming, to say the least. We never knew it would happen until digital clutter became an important topic.

Since we spend most of our time in the digital world, doesn't it make sense to keep our digital lives decluttered as well? Doesn't it make sense to keep our devices, which make our lives so much easier, as smooth-functioning as possible? How much of the things (documents, files, and folders) saved up in your digital space do you actually need? When did you last do a cleanup of your phone or computer?

Apart from the clutter on our digital devices, there is also clutter that can form from our overdependence on these devices. We spend hours plugged into these gadgets that they now define our happy and sad moments. Shut down your computer or phone and do something more physically or mentally demanding. Even if you work from a laptop most of the time, set out at least one hour per day to do something different like reading a book, taking a walk, talking to another human or even talking to yourself. Live in the real world, not just the digital world.

## The Principles of Digital Minimalism

- **Your devices should make your life easier not harder**

That's why they were invented in the first place, after all. Our phone and our computer should be helping our lives function more smoothly, with more ease. They should be helping us navigate obstacles, not creating more. You're not living by this principle if you find huge chunks of your time taken up by your device. Consider if the time you spend on your device is more than the time saved through its functional features.

- **Usage of your device should be intentional not addictive**

How often do you pick up your phone out of habit and anxiety, and not because you mean to carry out a specific action? There's a difference between opening your device to send an email and opening your device because you need to do something, anything, with your hands. Try to only use your device if there is something very specific you need it for.

- **Always put people before machines**

This one should be a given, but it's not, to so many people. We always think we're connecting with people because we're talking to them on the internet; while that's true sometimes, we also tend to ignore the people that are right in front of us to do this. Is your addiction to your phone getting in the way of your everyday interactions? How many times do you find yourself scrolling while you're in the company of someone who is trying to talk to you? Never let your machines take over.

## Important Advice for Defeating Digital Clutter

1.      **E-mails**: A cluttered inbox is enough to overwhelm you, when all you're trying to do is check up on your latest messages. The problem worsens when you have multiple emails for different purposes. If that is the case, then take it one email at a time.

## Minimalism & Decluttering

First, go through the different categories (your inbox, outbox, drafts, sent mail, etc.) and delete everything you do not need a record of. It is a tedious job, but it is worth it. You will find mail that has been there for years and mail that you replied to a long time ago. Work on your contact lists. Which services send you the most emails and why? Do you find the emails helpful in any way or do they just drive you to purchase things you don't need? If this adds to clutter, then unsubscribe, block, or delete.

Adopt a new habit of checking through your mail once in the morning and once in the evening, instead of doing so at random intervals. This way, digital clutter doesn't build up. Declutter your inbox of unnecessary emails every day so that clutter doesn't begin to build up again. Each week, run through your sent emails and delete those that need to be deleted. Cultivate these habits and practices, and make sure you don't fall back into old habits of ignoring digital clutter in your electronic mail.

**2.     Social Media:** Social media clutter can manifest itself in a variety of ways. First, there is an accumulation of unnecessary friends and people on your 'following' list. Sometimes you go online and see posts from people that you barely remember how you met. Sometimes you may feel this blanket of guilt coming over you as you unfriend or delete some contacts, but there is no good reason for this. This is a healthy habit for your digital life. There is no need to keep in contact with someone you barely know, especially if what they post is annoying or irrelevant to your life. Delete them and don't feel bad,

Cleaning up your social media accounts on various platforms will help set your priorities straight and feed you with relevant information, pictures, and status updates that you actually care about. Your mind also benefits from this because it will have lesser visual clutter to deal with, and it can focus on what you like.

The same method can be applied across all social media platforms. Streamline all your subscriptions and follow the necessary pages.

Connect your accounts across platforms to make your internet experience flow with ease.

Lastly, don't get consumed by social media. These platforms, even with all their numerous benefits, eat your time up. Don't spend more than ten minutes at a time on each platform. Do what you have come to do and leave. You are only allowed to spend more time than normal if you are running a Twitter advocacy group or making money from running Facebook ads. If it doesn't benefit you emotionally, mentally, or financially then you have no reason to spend more than an hour per day scrolling through an app.

3. **YOUR COMPUTER OR LAPTOP**

Most computer systems are digital junkyards. Is yours one of those? Only you can answer. The decluttering process starts by cleaning up your desktop. Think about your desktop as your parking lot or driveway. It is an introduction to your digital home. In fact, by merely looking at the level of organization on some desktops, I can tell how organized the owners are. There are many desktop icons that you don't use. Delete them: shortcuts, folders, and files. If there are documents that you still feel will be important to you in the future, you have the option of backing it up on cloud storage. But be careful, so your cloud storage doesn't suffer from clutter transfer. Only back up the files that you will definitely need in the future.

Keep all icons arranged at the left side of the desktop and ensure that they don't take up more than three rows at a time. If there are files that you reopen occasionally, put them in a folder and name them. Sort everything on your desktop by type.

Next, uninstall any programs that you rarely use. Free up space on your hard drive so your system can operate smoothly. Ensure that every single application installed on your system is one that is used frequently, not just eating space for no reason.

## Minimalism & Decluttering

Focus on categorizing your documents into relevant folders so that it will be easier to find each of them when they are needed. You will need concentration for this one and perhaps a pen and book to jot down the name of each new folder and the files in them. With your documents neatly organized in your computer, it will be easier for you to navigate through your system. The goal is to get through each folder and get rid of the excess and unnecessary documents.

Maintain the decluttered state of your computer by constantly deleting unnecessary files you don't need. Become a gatekeeper and keep track of all downloaded files. Keep them organized in the download folder so they can be deleted easily when the time comes.

# CHAPTER EIGHT - PERFECTING THE MINIMALISM EXPERIENCE

Minimalism is not just a lifestyle; it is an experience. Everything that we do contributes to the overall journey. These are the experiences that you should seek out, the experiences you should spend your money when you're not spending on useless stuff. Possessions and property gratify the body while worthy experiences delight the soul and mind. The nourishment of the soul and mind is important for the wellbeing of the body. That is why it is impossible to be attracted to an insane person, no matter how beautiful their bodies look.

Stocking our lives and homes with the latest gadgets seems satisfying because it provides you with the thrill of a brand new purchase, but this only lasts for a short period. The thrill dies off, and you are left in the same place you once found yourself: searching for another item to give you the same thrill. The cycle goes on, and you're never more satisfied than you were before. There are better ways for you to spend your money.

## Why We Need Experiences More Than Material Things

Money spent on experience is money spent nurturing the soul. The joy gotten from experiences lasts longer than the fleeting joy from purchasing stuff. This is why:

a. **Experiences help to solidify your own purpose and passions**

Everything that you do and spend money on should influence your future and propel you towards your purpose and passions in life; material possessions rarely compel you to do this. If you're obsessed with mountaineering, owning a hundred books on the topic or a dozen mountaineering outfits can never be equated to actually going on a mountaineering expedition. Material possessions will only fuel your imagination in regards to the experience, but the experience is what actually fuels your soul and satisfies you. This is why people go on road trips to see the country for themselves, not through pictures. This is why people go to music festivals; to see their favorite artists perform in person and not just listen to the same old recording.

### b. Shared experiences can foster relationships

An experience shared is a part of you shared. It's as simple as that. It is a bond that remains as long as both parties are alive. Have you ever caught yourself just smiling because the memory of a shared experience has come to your mind? It is a wonderful feeling, isnt it? Experiences shared with people made them closer to you. Think about all the close friendships you have and try to figure out what makes the friendship strong. The chances are high that those friendships blossomed over time because of a powerful shared experience or a series of shared experiences. Once you meet up with people you have shared your experiences with, there is never a dull moment. There are plenty of memories shared between the two parties, and conversations can last hours.

### c. Experiences introduce you to new things

A life without new experiences is a boring life devoid of learning and expansion of the mind Experiences can teach you the importance of life and friendship, and they can give you a changed, brand new perspective on the world. Everyone who has ever experienced real and transformative change did so because of one singular experience. Everyday people are discovering their purpose in life because of experiences, something they would have never known if they had chased possessions instead.

### d. Craving experiences will eliminate worries associated with buying stuff

In an earlier chapter, we established the degree of anxiety and worry that comes with purchasing new stuff. What if I was ripped off? What if I get robbed? What if this iPhone I bought for $999 suddenly drops into a bucket of water? The 'what ifs' are numerous and they make you paranoid. It takes up so much mental energy that you become stressed. That is not to say that you should never buy new things and spoil yourself once in a while, but seeking out experiences will greatly reduce these worries. Once you have some money saved up and have gotten your supplies ready, you can make plans and go after any experiences without worry. Your experience can never be taken away from you. Once you get it, it is yours forever, unlike all your material possessions.

## Experiences that are Better Than Any Material Object You Can Buy

### 1. Travel

How long have you remained in the current city or town you live in? A lot of people are comfortable staying in one place for more than a decade without crossing the borders. Just because your place of worship, a shopping mall, school, library and possibly a cinema are available where you reside doesn't mean there's no reason to venture out. Social media has made this situation worse since you can stay in your room and feel like you've traveled across the world through the internet. But there is more to the world than the city you live in. Go out and see for yourself. Don't depend on the pictures.

The feeling of being in a different country, experiencing their culture, and learning their stories is unparalleled. You can eat their local cuisine and learn a new language. You can even travel to the next city and take pictures of beautiful sights on your way there. Visit a relative and spend the night with them. Store the memories from your journeys and expand your mind. You need not travel far; just travel somewhere.

### 2. Festivals

Festivals bring passionate and excited people from everywhere to engage in a shared experience. Going to festivals with your friends is a great way to bond and meet new people. Even if you get lost and wander to the other side of the festival grounds, there is always a new experience waiting for you. Most of the people that go to festivals are people that share the same passions as you and meeting them will ignite your passion with even brighter flames.

Festivals are filled with culture, life, music, art, and people. There is always something to captivate you, no matter your interests are. Festivals are events where you can be yourself and express your individuality, no matter how weird. There are so many kinds of festivals you can enjoy. Music festivals are by far the most common, but there are also literary festivals and cultural festivals. Try them all!

### 3. A Weekend Getaway with Friends

You can plan this. All you need to do is to pick a location and travel there with friends. The main thing here is not the destination, but the journey itself. Arriving at your intended location will be fun too, but there's also nothing like getting together with friends and the laughter you share along the way. You don't even have to spend the night, wherever it is you travel to. You can go there in the morning, spend some time and be back by dinnertime.

For example, if you have friends who are art enthusiasts, you can plan to go to a museum or an art exhibition. Savor your experience by allowing yourself to be fully engaged in the program at hand. Or you could go on a hiking trip with friends and you could even camp out in the woods, if you're the outdoorsy type.

The beauty of going on such trips is the uncertainty that awaits you. You never know who or what you will meet, the humor you will find, or the stories that will be shared and created. These are the experiences from which life is truly made. One day, when you think back on your life, this is what you will remember.

### 4. Learn something new and exciting

The process of introducing your mind to something new will enhance the quality of your life and refine your mind. Your confidence levels will see a boost once you have success with your learning process. As we get older, our minds weaken because we no longer approach new activities or challenges with the same zest of our younger years. This is because we feel more tired and less motivated, not because we are less capable. The mind is always in search of new things to delve deeply into. If you keep on feeding it with routine or the same old information you already know, it keeps on getting weaker and loses its ability to stretch outwards.

It is also incredibly fun to learn new things. Don't see it as an activity you are 'bad' at, but an activity that you can learn from, that can show you a whole new side of the world. So many possibilities open up to you when you decide to grab the bull by the horns and learn something exciting. The process of discovery is filled with so much excitement. It can also be unexpectedly rewarding; you may find that your newfound skills open doors to a promotion or a new vocation entirely.

## The Experiences that Make Far Better Gifts than 'Stuff'

We're so attached to the expectation of showing up with a material object in hand, wrapped and ribbon-tied, ready to be opened. The world has fed us the idea that this is what we need to do to celebrate someone. We need a physical representation of our joy, our celebratory spirit. It's time to change this approach. There are many experiences we can gift our loved ones that are far more fun or special than a material object. They may even like it a lot more. Think of the clutter in your home, that heap of stuff that consists of bad gifts that you can't throw away. Don't add to someone else's clutter pile! Consider gifting these experiences:

### 1. Cooking Classes

Not only do cooking classes teach you valuable skills, they are also incredibly fun! Cooking without having to clean up afterwards? Yes, please! There are classes that teach a range of different cuisines. For something fun, baking desserts is always a great choice. Look online to find classes in your area.

### 2. A Spa Day or In-Home Massage

Why get someone a bottle of lotion or fragrant oil when you can buy them the experience of someone actually using it on them? It's a far better gift, if you ask me. Purchase a gift card for a local spa or arrange to have a masseuse come to their house. Everyone loves to feel pampered.

### 3. A Concert Ticket

Whoever it is you're buying a gift for definitely has a favorite musician or artist. See if this singer or band is on tour in the state any time soon. Oftentimes people miss this opportunity because they never think to check if their favorite artist is on tour. Even if they're absolute favorite will not be playing, something similar will also be enjoyable.

### 4. A Restaurant Gift Card

Many fabulous restaurants offer gift cards for this exact purpose. Treat someone you know to a fantastic dinner. Everyone enjoys a fantastic meal, especially when they aren't paying for it. This gift will not create clutter and it will fill their bellies.

### 5. Tickets to a Play or Musical

What's wonderful about this gift is that everyone enjoys theatre, but people will rarely buy themselves tickets to a performance. Yet once you're there, you get swept up in what an enthralling experience it is. You always enjoy it more than you think you will. Gift someone this experience because they are bound to have a great time.

### 6. Yoga Classes

Many yoga studios or instructors will offer a set number of classes for a discounted price. Consider treating someone you know to body-nourishing yoga, especially if you think exercise will benefit them. When someone buys us a gift, we feel like we have to make good use of it or they'll bad. Take advantage of this for something that will truly benefit your friend or relative!

### 7. Rosetta Stone

One of the best ways to learn a new language is with the program Rosetta Stone. If you know your friend or relative has a fascinating with a particular culture or country, gift them the experience of learning the language of that place. People rarely think to do this, but once they are given the opportunity, they are grateful for it.

### 8. Membership Programs

This may sound vague, but that's only because of just how much there is to choose from. When you gift someone a membership program, you are expanding their lifestyle. Get them a gym or museum membership. Or perhaps, a yearly pass to their favorite national park or amusement park. Most of these places allow you to buy a yearly pass. One thing is for sure: everyone will love this gift.

### 9. Free Babysitting

Do you know someone with kids they desperately need a break from? Offer them free babysitting sessions. You could write this out on a card or piece of paper and make it look like an official ticket. Commit to any number of sessions that you think you can handle, e.g. two or three sessions will help a lot but will also prevent you from becoming overwhelmed. It's an unconventional gift but any tired parent will deeply appreciate this.

### 10. A Staycation

Why not?! If you know someone who needs to take time out to unwind and feel pampered, pay for a night at a local hotel. Ideally, it should be somewhere comfortable and beautiful. It should be somewhere they'll enjoy more than home. When we get out of our space, we feel more relaxed. I know for sure that one of your friends needs this. Consider gifting a staycation experience!

# Minimalism & Decluttering

# **CONCLUSION**

Congratulations on finishing this book! I know the ideas and information I've presented to you have inspired you to begin the decluttering process of your home. The message of minimalism is not preached often, but it should be. Wouldn't you agree? We live in a consumerist world, and some people even frown upon minimalism; don't allow their attitudes to influence you. Protect your minimalist mindset at all costs. Do not allow the things you have learned throughout this book to slip your mind. Once you finish this book, you may even come across an ad telling you to buy a new product right now. Before you consider making this purchase, remember these companies don't really care about you. They just want to sell their product, and they'll tell you anything to make that happen. You are the cow they are trying to milk.

The journey of minimalism is never an easy one. You will come across people who loathe or even despise you for living by a different philosophy. They do so out of their own ignorance. And there is little you can do about it, especially when they aren't willing to hear you out. It is only natural. We, humans, are always quick to condemn things we do not understand. People will jump to conclusions and suggest that you aren't materialistic simply because you are unsuccessful. Of course, you and I know that isn't the case. By now, you've come to a complete understanding of how our quality of life is not determined by how much we own. In fact, clutter and excess can get in the way of our emotional, mental, or professional progress - the real things that contribute to our quality of life.

As I said in the preceding chapters, find your tribe, the people that share your minimalist goals with you. In recent years the conversation about minimalism and decluttering has increased exponentially. Join the conversation on social media and fuel your drive. You will need all the encouragement you can get. You will certainly come across people who have struggled with the things you are struggling with now. They will help you out with any questions you may have, especially now that our journey in this book has come to an end.

The benefits of minimalism are numerous, as I have stated before: freedom from clutter, financial security, and above all, peace of mind. This freedom allows you to chase experiences with a deeper meaning and greater relevance to your goals. You will discover yourself for who you truly are and not what you own. Your confidence will see a big boost because you no longer depend on your possessions and property to determine your value.

It is up to you now. We have gone through all of the most important facets of minimalism: the major habits, the principles, decluttering procedures, tips to reduce mental, emotional, and digital declutter, and much more. It is now up to you to keep practicing and building your great minimalist habits until they come naturally to you. Discipline and consistency are the most important factors in practicing minimalism. Never let go of them. Stay alert of clutter monsters and starve them to death before they become a huge menace. I wish you luck on your minimalist journey!

# SIMPLE YET EFFECTIVE TIME MANAGEMENT STRATEGIES

*Get Things Done In Less Time And Develop Atomic Habits With Productivity Methods Use By Highly Successful People*

Time Management

# Table of Contents

**Introduction** ........................................................................... 96

**Chapter 1 – Stop Wasting Time** ........................................ 100

    The Importance of Time Management ............................... 100

    Signs You're Failing at Managing Your Time ................... 102

    The Reasons Why You're Failing ....................................... 107

    7 Big Myths About Time Management .............................. 109

**Chapter 2 - Getting Things Done 101** .............................. 112

    Essential Tips for Getting Things Done ............................. 112

    Essential Rules for Successful Time Management ............ 114

    5 Lesser-Known Productivity Hacks You Need to Know .. 120

**Chapter 3 - A Guide to Goal-Setting** ............................... 127

    All About the Goal-Setting Theory of Motivation ............ 127

    Goal-Setting Principles ....................................................... 128

    15 of the Best Tips for Effective Goal-Setting .................. 134

    8 Common Reasons Why To-Do Lists Fail ....................... 138

**Chapter 4 - The Secrets of Productivity** ......................... 142

    How to Prioritize When Everything Is Important ............. 142

    The Chunking Technique for Making Your Goals Achievable ... 150

    5 of the Biggest Productivity Killers and How to Overcome Them ................................................................................ 155

**Chapter 5 - Dealing with Distractions** ............................. 158

    The Difference Between Internal and External Distractions ... 158

    Types of Internal Distractions ............................................ 160

    13 Ways to Silence Internal Distractions ........................... 164

    6 Reliable Ways to Defeat External Distractions .............. 169

**Chapter 6 - Emulating Success** ........................................................ 173
   Goal Setting Examples from The Business Masters ................... 173
   13 Time Management Hacks of Successful People ..................... 176
   10 Morning Routines of Groundbreaking Entrepreneurs............. 180

**Chapter 7 - Regaining Control of The Future**............................ 184
   15 Effective Time Management Habits ......................................... 184
   Defeating Perfectionism Once and for All.................................... 188
   Tools and Techniques to Take Back Time for Good ................... 194

**Conclusion** ............................................................................................ 200

Time Management

# Introduction

The only resource you can't barter, buy or borrow is time. It doesn't even follow one of the fundamental laws of supply and demand: high demand causes supply to increase and meet the demand. While we all have access to the same amount of time each day —1,440 minutes — we use our time differently.

Your success or failure in life depends mainly on your time management capabilities. To be successful, you need to invest significant amounts of time to achieve your goal or improve your weaknesses. At certain seasons, I spent more time than my competitors so that I can have the edge over them in the marketplace. I didn't assume that I was mentally superior to my competitors; I only spent time more effectively to balance the playing field.

You need to spend balance the time you spend at home and the time you spend at work. If not, you will be successful in one and be a failure in the other. Fear not; this book will show you how to balance your work and home effectively. I congratulate you on investing in your life and success by reading this book.

If you are reading this, it's probably because:

- You want to be confident that you can take proper care of yourself and your family
- You desire long-lasting success in your career and personal life
- You want your friends and families to be proud of you and your accomplishments

## Time Management

Here's what you're probably doing right in your life:

Since you are serious about improving your life experience, you are possibly implementing these basic career success strategies:

- You ensure that your performance at work exceeds the expectations of your bosses
- You arrive early and when needed, work overtime
- You are continually improving yourself to improve your work performance
- You seek mentors and network with your peers

The truth is, none of these actions will lift you to the personal or professional lifestyle you desire and deserve. Why? Let me explain:

For all things to function correctly, there has to be a balance. Let's use the washing machine's spin cycle as an illustration. When there are too many towels on one side of the tub, it slams, bangs and vibrates. If you don't fix it in time, the bearings will break, and the repairs can be expensive.

Your life can be likened to the washing machine. If you only focus and implement the necessary success steps of most people, you will achieve the same level of success as them. Thus, you may never accomplish everything you want or need in life. Your life will be completely imbalanced.

Over time, you will start getting drained spiritually, physically and emotionally. Consequently, you may begin to experience social problems, relationship problems, and health problems such as depression, diabetes, heart diseases, and high blood pressure. When you continuously live a life out of balance, you may never achieve your set goals or ambitions.

For centuries, the Chinese have known and have been implementing the yin and yang principle. The principle states that "two halves that complement each other produces wholeness." The keyword here is "wholeness." The two halves are your mind and your body; they work together to make your life whole.

If your life is not whole, you are not different from the wet towels swinging around the washing machine.

Let me tell you a secret: every successful person you have met and will ever meet are masters of productivity. If an expert should hand you the complete guide to success through proper time management, would you implement the steps in the guide?

- Will you use the secrets to increase your productivity and raise your success level?
- If you discover the productivity secrets of the most successful people, will you implement these secrets?
- I am willing to show you exactly what I do daily to consistently achieve my career and personal goals to live the kind of lifestyle you seek. Are you willing to follow these steps faithfully?

If your answer is yes to these three questions, then, you are ready to reach a new level of success with *Time Management: Proven Steps and Strategies for Managing Your Time Efficiently and Effectively.* This book

- Isn't just some rah-rah cheerleader guide that excites you with biographies and quotes of successful people. You won't find the typical "secrets to time management" that are copied and pasted articles from the internet and thrown together like some cheap pulp fiction novel.
- Details my exact daily actions and by all means, I am a successful and fulfilled person
- Shows you how to prioritize when everything is important
- Delves into the techniques for making your goals achievable

- Takes you deep into the biggest productivity killers and how to overcome them
- Helps you with ways to silence internal distractions
- Tells you reliable ways to defeat external distractions
- Contains goal-setting examples from the business masters
- Discusses time management hacks of successful people
- Takes you deep into the morning routines of groundbreaking entrepreneurs

I won't call this book a life-changing book. I will instead call it a life-enhancing book. With it, you start with the life you've built and elevated it to the levels you desire by implementing the exact steps of truly successful people.

In this book, you will find the precise information you need. You can start from the first page or read on topics that cause you the most challenge. I can assure you that this book will help you to maximize the scant 24 hours we all have per day.

For instance, you can check out chapter one for signs that suggest your time management sucks! Also, in chapter three, you will discover common reasons why you can't do anything with your to-do lists.

The point is, regardless of the chapter you choose to start reading, you will discover lots of valuable steps you can implement. Thus, you can increase your performance without increasing your work hours.

# Chapter 1 – Stop Wasting Time

## The Importance of Time Management

By definition, time management is a process of organizing and planning your time between specific activities to achieve efficiency.

Time is valuable to us whether or not we assign a dollar value to it. Think about the number of times you complained about having insufficient time to reach a goal or complete a task during this past week. If you don't fully understand why it's crucial for you to manage your time better, then, taking measures such as downloading time management apps, creating lists or adjusting your sleep time won't help you to solve your problems. First, take a look at the big picture to understand what you will gain from managing your time effectively. Here are eight critical reasons why you need to manage your time effectively:

### 1. Prevent procrastination

You leave no room for procrastination when you practice proper time management. You will become more self-disciplined as you become better at managing your time. Thus, you can become self-disciplined in other areas of your life where you lack discipline.

### 2. Find the time to relax

Due to family responsibilities, errands and jobs, the majority of us don't get sufficient time to relax and unwind. We struggle to find just 10 minutes to sit down and do nothing. With proper time management practices, you will get more done during the day and create the time to relax, unwind and prepare for a good night's sleep later in the day.

### 3. Avoid stress

It's easy to feel rushed and overwhelmed when you are not in control of your time. Thus, you will start struggling to complete your tasks. Imagine you were making frantic efforts to finish a project to avoid missing a close deadline. Then, your boss drops a new job on your desk and asks you how soon you can complete the new task. What will be your response?

However, when you can manage your time, you will complete most projects before their deadlines. You can adequately estimate the period you will use to complete a task and be confident in meeting deadlines.

### 4. Take advantage of learning opportunities

You become more valuable to your employer as you improve your repertoire. But if you don't have the time to enhance your knowledge, how can you become more relevant to your employer? Once you practice excellent time management skills, you can take advantage of great learning opportunities around you.

It doesn't mean going back to obtain additional certificates. Learning can be as simple as volunteering to host your company's open house. It can also be having lunch with colleagues in other departments to gain further insights into what they do. When you have adequate knowledge about your company and your industry, you have a higher chance of moving up the corporate ladder quickly.

### 5. Be in control of your life

Rather than following others blindly, time management allows you to control your life the way you want it. Thus, you make more sound decisions and accomplish more every day. Hence, the leaders in your industry will start seeking your help to get things done. With this increased exposure, you become perfectly placed for advanced opportunities.

### 6. Improve your decision-making

Regardless of the time management techniques you adopt, one significant side benefit of good time management practice is that you start making better decisions. When you don't have the time to consider your options before making a decision, you jump into conclusions and make poor decisions. Through effective time management, you feel more in control and can thoroughly examine your options before making a decision.

### 7. Improve your focus

When you are in control of your time, your concentration improves, and your efficiency is enhanced. Thus, you can complete your daily tasks quickly and effectively.

Do you want to consistently complete more tasks than anybody else? Do you seek promotion or awards? Then, you need to find the means to manage your time.

## Signs You're Failing at Managing Your Time

Do you:

- Constantly have more to do than the time to them?
- Not rest from the time you wake up to the time you sleep in the night?
- Always feel tired after each day's work?

One vital attribute of a skilled manager is effectiveness. If you intend to accomplish a goal and you are not completing the right tasks to accomplish that goal, you won't accomplish it.

Here are some of the most common signs that you're failing at managing your time:

## Time Management

### 1. No task delegation

You need to identify tasks that you can delegate, automate or outsource and remove them from your workload. Here are examples of tasks that you can delegate:

- Your most time-consuming tasks. These tasks could be customer research, developing a marketing strategy, collation and presentation of data, traffic generation and improvement of click-through rate.
- Tasks others might enjoy. You may have become bored with a task after completing it repeatedly. Hence, if you think some of your colleagues could enjoy it, delegate such task to them. Also, if a colleague should volunteer for a task, allow him to perform it.
- Tasks in which teammates have better skills. Devote your time to other things and allow teammates with better skills to handle tasks that suit their skills and abilities. Avoid being the competition for your teammates. If they are better at a task than you, let them have it.
- Fun tasks. Your teammates are likely to take offense when you perform all the enjoyable tasks and ask them to deal with the tedious tasks. Why keep the fun to yourself? Let them share in the fun.
- Regular tasks. These are recurring tasks (weekly or monthly) and things that must be done after completing a project.

### 2. Agreeing to everyone

If you continuously agree to do things for everyone, excluding your loved ones, you won't have the time to improve your life or have the time for your loved ones. If you're always helping others without working on the important tasks assigned to you, you will constantly have an excessive workload. Being assertive and learning to say "no" is one of the best ways to improve your time management.

While it is great to help your teammates at work, it should only be an occasional occurrence. If it becomes a regular occurrence, you're doing their job for them and no longer helping them. They need to figure out how to work without continually requesting for your help. Otherwise, they also have time management problems, and they need to deal with it fast.

## 3. Indecision

Have you experienced spending lots of time to consider various options but still can't make a decision? It is a sign that you have poor time management. This sign is related to having ill-defined goals. When your goals are clearly defined, you have a basis for choosing your next most important task at any given time. The next task is often chosen based on the ROI. For example, assuming you are to choose between two 1-hour tasks. Task A will give you an ROI of $100, while task B will provide you with an ROI of $150. If your goal is to make more money, your obvious choice is task B.

Tasks vary in time of execution and costs. Also, you may have restrictions on the next task to be performed due to resources available, energy levels and other factors. After a clearly-defined goal, here's one question you can ask to make an easy decision on the next task to perform. "Using the time and resources currently available to me, what's the most important task I can complete?"

## 4. Perfectionism

When tasks take too long to achieve or even fail because you wanted to ensure that everything is perfect, you are a poor time manager. When you are overwhelmed by the need for perfection, you fail to realize that very few tasks are performed flawlessly in reality. By making unrealistic demands from your teammates, your desire for perfection can destroy your relationships with them. If you berate your colleagues when they fail to reach your perfect standards, you will struggle to find colleagues willing to work with you.

Since you can't maintain cordial working relationships with your colleagues, you will always have time management problems. You can't do everything by yourself. You should realize that perfection is impossible and, most times, unnecessary. Only demand the best from your colleagues for each task. Then, using the feedback from completed tasks, you can make the necessary improvements.

Bear in mind that a perfect job that never gets completed is useless compared to an average job that meets the deadline.

## 5. Productivity decline

When you manage your time poorly, you miss deadlines; you have an increase in backlog and your productivity declines. Time management and energy management are equally important. If you can't do anything with your energy levels, merely organizing your time is a waste of effort. Once you have reduced energy levels, you start having poor time management. Hence, you are under intense pressure to complete tasks without missing the required deadline. This even sucks up more of your energy levels.

Track your energy levels when you struggle to find the cause of your poor time management. Seek ways to improve your energy management.

## 6. Ill-defined goals

You can only prioritize when you have clearly defined goals. Consequently, you can complete your tasks on time. Each goal should have a clearly defined outline - what to achieve, when to achieve it and the order of importance. You need to set clearly-defined goals around your schedule of activities. Thus, you gain clarity on what needs to be done and when you need to do it.

According to the 80/20 principle, not all tasks carry equal importance. On average, 20% of your efforts will be responsible for 80% of your results. The smallest percentage of the tasks you perform will be responsible for the most significant percentage of the results you will achieve. You can only identify the 80/20 tasks when you have clearly-defined goals. A side benefit is that you will eliminate time-consuming tasks.

## 7. Finding excuses

The pressure of failing to meet a deadline makes you impatient. Hence, you start finding reasons for failing to complete your deadlines. Most people attribute their poor time management to people, technology or both. But the truth is, if you have failed to manage your time correctly, people and technology cannot help you. Ensure that you are only working on essential tasks that you can complete using the time and resources available to you.

You will ruin your ability to focus on the crucial task by adding an unneeded deadline. Assuming there is a task that needs to be completed by the close of business tomorrow, but you decided to shift the deadline to close of business today without being pressured to do so. You would only be putting yourself under unnecessary pressure and rushing to complete the task. While on the contrary, it would have been best for you to spread the task's process between today and tomorrow.

## 8. Hastiness

When you rush tasks, it is a sign that you don't have enough time for these tasks or meet the expectations of these tasks. While some tasks require some rush, you shouldn't be rushing to complete all your assigned tasks. You should have ample time between tasks to deal with unanticipated circumstances.

For example, a previous meeting exceeded its allotted time. If you leave every task to the last minute, you will continuously be in a rush. What you fail to realize is that if meeting A runs late, meeting B will start late, and you have to spend your rest period to complete your assigned task for the day.

### 9. Tardiness

When you can't allot sufficient time to appointments or tasks, you are unable to complete these tasks or fail to meet appointments. Your peers assume you are irresponsible. In some cases, your tardiness may be a motivation problem. You can't motivate yourself to get out of bed and do what you're supposed to do. One primary reason for your motivation problem may be a misalignment between your goals and your time management objectives.

Your best option is to prioritize your goals and manage your time to achieve these goals. When you schedule a goal that isn't your priority, you lose the motivation to be punctual since you fail to realize the importance of the task. Hence, you come up short at tasks without feeling any remorse, and you're known for your frequent poor time management practice.

The truth is, when you are punctual, it shows you respect your colleagues. The reverse is also true: when you are late, it is a sign that you disrespect your colleagues. Rather than being late for tasks that seem unimportant to you, you can decline to undertake the task.

## The Reasons Why You're Failing

There are times we struggle to control our daily affairs despite our best efforts to efficiently organize our time, stay ahead of schedule or complete tasks successfully. Rather than creating additional to-do lists, you must identify the source of time management issues. Where your time slipping away, and what is are you doing wrong?

Let's take a look at eight reasons why you're failing at time management:

## 1. No plan at all

You need a proper method to change something already in motion in your life. Don't expect everything to fix itself. Create a timetable that makes you accountable for every hour of your day. Don't deviate from your daily plan, refer to it and review it. Thus, you can start developing and incorporating new habits into your day.

## 2. Procrastination

Start implementing your scheme immediately. Don't wait for the new month, Sunday or the next milestone in your life before making a change. The main idea is for you to act on the plan.

## 3. No grace

Since you're not perfect, there are times you will mess up. However, it doesn't mean you're a failure, or your hard work isn't paying off. So, give yourself the grace to get up the next day and be better.

## 4. Lack of accountability

Ask a trusted colleague to make you accountable for your daily actions. If you are late, mention it to the trusted colleague. Then, make a plan for what happens when you fail to meet your set expectations.

## 5. No motivation

The comments from your coworkers shouldn't motivate you. Decide on your motivation and ensure it's the right kind of motivation. Examples of strong motivators are personal development, excellence and well-being. Changes you make for your well-being will become a lifestyle change, but changes made for someone else won't last.

## 6. Making unnecessary changes

Concentrate on one specific goal at a time. If your objective is to get to work on time, identify the cause of your lateness to work. Then, eliminate it. Make it a priority to determine the necessary changes you need to make. Making unnecessary changes won't lead to new habits. For instance, spending two hours on Facebook early in the morning can cause you to be late for work. You can switch that up and spend two hours on Facebook the previous night. If the changes are necessary, make them a priority.

## 7. Unrealistic expectations

Don't over-expect. If you usually wake up at 7:45 am and get to work by 8.15 instead of 8 am, then, you can't suddenly start waking up at 5 am. It won't work that way. Your best option is to start learning how to wake up at 7 am. Then, slowly work your way up till you start waking up at 5:30 am.

## 8. Implementing a lot at once

One big mistake when addressing an issue in your life is to make a long list of things to change. Then, trying to take action on all these things at once on the next day. That's an entirely wrong approach. Your first step is to learn how to get out of bed on time. Then, seek to achieve the next goal. Over time, you would have developed new habits.

# 7 Big Myths About Time Management

In today's always-on business world, time management is crucial than ever. Though most professionals offer various tips to prioritize and balance work tasks and the home front, most of these tips are myths and poor advice that could have a negative impact than a positive one.

Here are the top seven myths you shouldn't buy about time management:

### 1. "Budget your time."

Don't be surprised when your budget gets shot 15 minutes into the day. Instead, create regular chunks of time in which you will make sufficient progress before moving to the next goal. During these chunks of periods, don't take calls, answer emails or check your social media page. Doing this helps you to avoid random interruptions rather than 'got a minute' meetings.

### 2. "Plan your day."

This was the mantra of time management. However, you may never get close to your long-term goals by using daily plans. Why? You finish each day with additional to-dos which you add to the next day's list until you give up on your long-term goals. A simple and effective solution is to include your long-term goals into your weekly plans.

### 3. "A detailed task list is essential to manage your time."

It is more important to structure your tasks in line with your strategic objectives rather than just listing them. You can become a master of time management by using 15 minutes before your bedtime the previous day to plan your next day to meet a defined expectation. You increase your decision-making and productivity by limiting your planning time.

### 4. "A structured day means a well-managed time."

For optimum results, time management, efficiency, effectiveness and productivity depend on each individual. There is no one-size-fits-all proposition. You need to find out what works for you.

### 5. "There's always time for your priorities."

You can still feel stressed despite knowing your priorities and aligning your activities with them. Bear in mind that you can only change how you feel about the time you have, but you can't change the time. It will always feel stressful to think you have insufficient time. Instead, tell yourself, "I have all the time I need to accomplish my desires." by doing this, you are more present and open to new, different solutions, you become more present and feel calmer. Thus, you can get more done.

## 6. "Schedule your hardest tasks first."

A recipe for procrastination is to attempt a tough task when you are rock bottom energy levels. If your energy is typically high at midnight, focus on the most challenging projects during this time. If you're usually flat on Thursday afternoon, schedule less important meetings for that day.

## 7. "Better time management is a result of better task management."

Though I am a fan of time blocking for managing priorities, I still believe that we need to make intentional choices on where to focus our energy before we can have proper time management. Since our choices define our priorities, we need to make better choices to have better time management.

# Chapter 2 - Getting Things Done 101

## Essential Tips for Getting Things Done

Getting things done, or GTD, is a reasonably simple method contrary to what you may think. It involves using simple rules to manage a few lists. Anyone, regardless of their background, can understand and apply these rules.

However, you need to develop at least one of the three habits for getting things done. Hence, the complicated part of GTD is in practice and not getting things done. Here those three habits:

### 1. Keep your head empty

*"An empty mind is open to everything and ready for anything."* - Shunryu Suzuki

David Allen is the author of *Getting Things Done - The Art of Stress-Free Productivity*. He recommends that you need to capture the essential elements necessary for you to get things done. Then, keep it out of your head in a reliable system where you can review it at any time.

Everything here includes what you have to do soon or someday (the big things and the small things). Some may be part of your work, while others may be part of your personal life. However, they should be the ones you regard as the most important and the ones you consider as less important.

Here are six reasons why you need to include everything:

- All things require your steady and conscious attention.
- You waste time and incur stress when you think of the same things repeatedly. Once you put them into a trusted system and out of your mind, you do them effortlessly.

- You have clarity on the number of things you need to do
- Since you are not distracted by indefinite stuff in your mind, your concentration increases.
- You can reject the things you shouldn't, and don't want to do since you have a clear idea of your commitments.
- You can start using your mind for creative activities rather than trying to remember things.

## 2. Be decisive

*"When there is no next action; there is an infinite gap between current reality and what has to be done."* - David Allen

Change is inevitable whether we like it or not. Hence, you need the discipline to decide the next best course of action. You must have a clear idea about your commitment to each activity. Then, make a decision about such a thing.

For your organization to work smoothly, you must empty your inbox regularly. Define and clarify each thing you have captured previously. Also, you need to decide what you will do with each item. What are your reasons for doing it?

When you know your reasons, you:

- You become aware of the reality and focus on the essential things rather than being carried away by what's urgent. Thus, your anxiety levels are at the barest minimum
- Are in full control because you know what to do and when to do it
- Experience a feeling of relief each time you make a decision. Also, you are not under any intense pressure since you have a clearer perspective about your goals
- Have higher self-esteem since you are responsible for your actions

- Are more productive since you have a reinforced ability to get things done.

### 3. Update your system regularly

*"You have train yourself to see the forest and the tree before your knowledge can be productive"* - Peter F. Drucker

You need to review your system regularly to make it useful. Reflect on the essential things in your life, work, current projects, and next actions frequently. Here are a few crucial reasons why you need to review your system regularly:

- A complete review reveals what you are not doing that you should be doing
- Since each action has a clearly defined step, missing one step would affect your result.

# Essential Rules for Successful Time Management

It is an open secret that effective time management has loads of benefits. How many times have you heard that better time management reduces stress, saves time, and boosts efficiency? I am sure it's more than you can count. But the truth is, we often struggle to practice effective time management

We procrastinate, then, when we realize that the deadline is close, we start rushing to meet with the timeline. No one has the power to slow downtime, but you can get the most of your day by managing your time correctly.

Here are some proven time management tips to become a master of time management:

## 1. Batch them together

Batch related work together. For example, schedule a specific period to answer your emails and phone calls. Don't handle these tasks or similar tasks throughout the day. Different projects require a different thought process. Hence, batching together related tasks prevents your brain from switching to different thought processes each time you have to accomplish a different job. Batching helps your mind to eliminate the time it takes for your brain to reorient to accommodate the different new task.

## 2. Focus on the important aspects

This tip is a credit to Leo Babauta of the Zen Habits blog. According to him, you have to spend a few minutes to understand what needs to be done then, focus on those crucial things alone. Thus, you make every action count and create more value. In this case, less is not more; less is better.

## 3. Telecommute

Based on research, the average American commutes for at least 25 minutes. It is even predicted that this average time will increase in the nearest future. Add this time to the time it takes you to be prepared for your commute. Then, you will discover that you are wasting considerable time going to and coming back from work. The solution: if it's remotely possible with your job, try telecommuting at least once per week. You will save several hours per week which you can use for other productive means.

## 4. Make the best of your wait time

By all standards, I'm a patient person. But I can't stand waiting knowing I can spend that time more productively. Hence, I think of the best ways to spend that time. For example, if I'm waiting to see my doctor, I could create a blueprint for an upcoming blog post, listen to a podcast, or read an inspirational book.

### 5. Incorporate support habits

Charles Duhigg wrote a book called *The Power of Habits,* where he defined keystone habits. These life-transforming habits include meditating, developing daily routines, tracking what you eat, and exercising. By incorporating these support habits into your daily routine, you will replace bad habits with good habits over time. Consequently, you are more focused, healthier, and a better manager of your time.

### 6. Don't be afraid to say "No."

While you don't want your colleagues to be angry with you, you have limited time just like everyone else. For example, if you don't have spare time, you shouldn't try helping your colleagues with their assigned tasks.

### 7. Maximize the use of Google Calendar

Though calendars have been a fundamental time management tool for a long time, online calendars have taken it to the next level. You can access an online calendar from multiple devices. Then, use that tool to schedule recurring events, create time blocks, set up reminders, easily schedule meetings, and appointments.

While I think Google Calendar is the best because it's the one I use, Apple Calendar and Outlook can serve the same purpose.

### 8. Schedule buffer time between tasks or meetings

It may seem like a good use of your time to jump to a new project immediately after completing a previous task. But it has an opposite effect; it clutters your mind. The human brain can only focus for at least 90 minutes at once.

Hence, you need time even if it's a few minutes to recharge your mind, refresh your body, and boost your brain. Walking and meditation are two proven ways to clear your mind and recharge.

Otherwise, you will struggle to focus or stay motivated. Based on my experience, a buffer time of 25 minutes between tasks is always ideal.

## 9. Alter your schedule

Altering your schedule can be a simple and effective solution to your time management struggles. For example, you can wake one hour earlier than your usual time. You can use this extra hour to work on side projects, check your emails, plan your day, exercise, or a combination of these tasks. Also, consider cutting down the amount of TV you watch and maintain the same wake-up routines during weekends.

## 10.     Stop half-work.

According to James Clear, author of the *New York Times* best-seller *Atomic Habits*: "In this age of constant distraction, it's easy to split our focus between societal demands and what we should do. Typically, we are trying to accomplish a task and at the same time checking our to-do lists, emails, and messages. Hence, we can't fully focus on the project we are trying to accomplish."

Here some of the examples he gave of what he called "half-work":

- Your mind is wandering to your email inbox while communicating on the phone
- Writing a report, then, stopping to check your phone for no reason
- Altering your workout routine because you watched a couple of YouTube videos

The point is, when you engage in half-work, it takes you twice the time to accomplish a task, and you will only achieve half the mission. Clear opined that the best solution to half-work is to focus on one project and complete it before thinking about or starting any other task.

For example, pick an exercise and focus on it alone for your workouts. Also, leave your phone in a separate room and devote a significant amount of time on a substantial project. Clear claims that "the best way to achieve deep, focused work and avoid half-work is to eliminate distractions."

## 11. List all measurable steps to complete a task

All goals and projects are a sum of small moving parts. Hence, you need to clearly define the small moving parts to accomplish a project or goal. A side benefit is that you are motivated by what you have achieved. Thus, you can become focused on what you're yet to accomplish.

When you experience interruptions, ensure you are not entirely carried away by the distraction. A proven way to avoid getting taken away by a distraction is to limit the number of tasks you are performing at a specific time.

## 12. Apply the Eisenhower principle

You need to identify the urgent and essential tasks from your to-do list before working on them. This concept was first coined by Dwight D. Eisenhower, the 34th US president.

- You achieve personal goals with important tasks
- You achieve immediate goals with urgent tasks. Typically, urgent tasks have immediate consequences but are associated with accomplishing another person's intent.

Eisenhower's principle suggests prioritizing tasks into four groups:

- Not urgent and not important: These are complete distractions. Avoid them.
- Urgent but not important: these are barriers to your tasks, and your co-workers mostly provide them. They seek your

## Time Management

help to accomplish their tasks. When this happens, you can suggest another competent person for them or say "No."

- Not urgent but important: These are tasks necessary to accomplish your goals. Thus, ensure you properly prepare for them.
- Urgent and important: These are the first tasks you should undertake every day. Some might be last-minute tasks, while others might be emergency tasks. With proper planning, you can prevent last-minute tasks. But you can't plan for emergency issues. Your best option is to allow a buffer time to deal with such problems. Including time slots for emergencies is one of the best ways to prioritize your tasks.

### 13. Apply the concept of leverage to complete your task

The smart use of leverage will help you to achieve the most significant returns with the least effort. Use the Pomodoro technique to avoid working overtime. This technique suggests that you "divide and structure your work into 25-minute sessions and a 5-minute break between the sessions."

For example, assuming you're working on a presentation and you've estimated that you need about 150 minutes to accomplish the task. Divide the task into six 25-minute sessions and a 5-minute break between them. Ensure that your sessions are not in conflict with other commitments or plans. Start working once the timer sets off after 25 minutes. Rest for 5 minutes after each session, then, repeat till you complete the sessions. Rest for 30 minutes after completing all the sessions.

### 14. Track your time

I have saved the best for the last. The first step to proper time management is to determine how you spend your time. You may believe you spend just 25 minutes on emails, while in reality, you spend more than 45 minutes on it per day.

Time apps such as my app calendar, Toggl, or RescueTime offers an easy way for you to track your time and activities weekly. Track your activities for next week, then, use the report to identify your time stealers and make appropriate adjustments.

## 5 Lesser-Known Productivity Hacks You Need to Know

As a live, breathing human being, there are times you will struggle with your productivity. Often, our inability to produce results consistently and repeatedly is one major thing that holds us back in life. For most of us, there are times we have peak productivity, but most times we have valley productivity. These are the main barriers to our life goals.

Before you can make significant progress in life, you must be productive consistently and repeatedly. You can't have five days of valley productivity and two days of high productivity in any given week. At the very least, you should have five days of high productivity and two days of valley productivity in any given week. However, we all struggle to be highly productive at all times.

Sometimes, we are on high productivity alert. At other times, something zaps our spirit, and our productivity declines. We either indulge in one of our preferred pleasures, or we hit one of life's stumbling blocks. Consequently, our relationships, health, careers, and finances suffer.

What's the solution?

First, you need to identify the impediments to your productivity. Examples of such obstacles include the inability to focus, lack of focus, poor time management skills, and procrastination. If you desire any significant, positive changes in your life, you must learn how to overcome these impediments consistently.

## What are productivity hacks?

Hacks are tricks, skills, or shortcuts that can improve your productivity. Bear in mind there are no new productivity hacks; there are only multiple workarounds for us to get and stay productive.

Here are the best five of such hacks:

## 1. Focus on small and fast wins

Trying to do many things all at once is a common mistake. Another usual error is taking on a huge project in one go. If you want to get things done, start by taking baby steps one at a time.

Split your most important goal into:

- Daily goals
- Weekly goals
- Monthly goals
- Quarterly goals
- Yearly goals

Then, always ask yourself: "What's that one step I will take today that will make me closer to my end goal?" Focus on small and fast wins; avoid dreaming about your big goal.

These small and fast wins will help you to achieve your big goal over time.

Example; big goal: Become a self-published author.

Since a typical book has about 300 pages, you need to a little over 75,000 words (an average of 250 words per page) for the 300 pages.

Breakdown: make it a habit to write 400 words per day rather than thinking about the end goal (75,000 words). Start with 100 words today, and by the end of next week, you must have written another 1,000 words. If you continue that way, you should complete your 300-page book within six months.

That's the magic that happens when you focus on small and fast wins.

## 2. Don't break the consistency

If you are trying to build a habit within 21 days because you read it or watched it somewhere, you are wrong. The truth is, it takes between 18 and 254 days to build a habit. The key to forming any pattern is consistency. A strong start but giving up too soon is one primary reason why most people are unable to build life-changing habits. If you fall into this category, then, apply the Jerry Seinfeld productivity hack. It's also known as the "don't break the chain" hack.

Here's an excerpt from an article on life hacker by Brad Isaac in which Jerry Seinfeld explains this hack:

"The best way to be the best comic is to create better jokes. Writing every day is the way to create better jokes. Use a unique calendar system as a leverage technique to pressure yourself to write. Get a wall calendar with a whole year on one page and hang it where it can be prominent. Then, use a big red magic marker to put a big red x over each day you perform your task. You should have a chain after a few days of consistent practice. The chain will keep growing, provided you keep at it. After a few weeks of consistency, you will be motivated to keep the chain growing. Thus, your only task is to avoid breaking the chain."

This hack is useful because it helps you to be consistent with your skill or talent.

The three steps to get started with this hack:

**Step 1:** Figure out your skill or learn it. You can choose to become a master at SEO, a highly sought-after programmer or an exceptional stand-up comedian. This is a vital step; don't skip it.

**Step 2:** Put up a one-year calendar on a prominent space in your home, office, or workplace.

**Step 3:** As you devote time to work on that skill, cross each day with a big x. Focus on lengthening the chain. Your only task is to avoid breaking the chain.

## 3. Use a standing desk

I know it seems crazy, but using a standing desk can improve your focus and productivity by up to 46%. New evidence by Texas A & M University research suggests that employees using standing desks are 46% more productive than those using the traditional seated desk configurations. Now, most hip office use standing desks. Also, FF Venture capital discovered that results in more active sharing of ideas. It is a well-known fact Thomas Jefferson, and a few other prominent individuals worked at standing desks for most days of their lives.

Other benefits of working at a standing desk at home or workplace include:

- Increased productivity. You won't check your inbox too frequently
- Calorie reduction. Using a standing desk exercises the significant muscles in your legs

- Improved focus. It is normal to feel a sense of urgency when standing. Thus, you are more focused and can complete tasks on time
- Improvements to your digestive health. A standing desk prevents you from sleeping at your desk. Thus, you experience less fatigue.

When you use standing desks, you have little or no urge to multitask, switch between websites, check email, and be distracted in any other way.

## How to get started:
- **Start in small cycles.** Rather than start working at your standing desk for straight hours. Start with baby steps. Start with 20 minutes per day, then increase this time gradually till you can ultimately spend your day on a standing desk
- **Use Pinterest** or similar sites to get creative ideas on setting up your standing desk
- **Take breaks.** Avoid stiffness or fatigue by consuming a cup of coffee, practicing squats or going for a short walk.

## 4. Implement the 2-minute rule

It is surprising to know that you can accomplish quite a lot within two minutes. The inclusion of mundane tasks in a daily to-do list is one of the reasons why 90% of people never achieve the tasks on their to-do lists. Thus, you need a systemic approach to tackling your to-do list. That systemic approach is the 2-minute rule.

By implementing the 2-minute rule, you focus on essential tasks and eliminate the unimportant tasks.

The 2-minute rule is split into two parts:

- Start and complete anything that can be accomplished within two minutes
- Start anything that takes more than two minutes to accomplish

## Part 1. Start and complete anything that can be accomplished within two minutes

Don't add this 2-minute task to your to-do list, don't procrastinate about it and don't outsource it. Do it immediately and forget about it. Tasks that fit into a 2-minute project include cleaning up clutter, sending that email, taking out the garbage, tossing the laundry in the washing machine, washing your dishes immediately after your meal.

With time, you will start uncovering more 2-minute tasks. Build and maintain excitement in your workday by ticking off this 2-minute task. There's a sense of accomplishment synonymous with getting things done. By micro-managing unimportant tasks through the 2-minute principle, you can manage your daily to-do lists with greater effectiveness.

## Part 2. Start anything that takes more than two minutes to accomplish

If you have 2-hour, 2-day, 2-week, or 2-month tasks, then, you may start wondering how to accomplish them down within two minutes. When you build momentum by accomplishing a 2-minute task, you feel better equipped to perform more significant tasks. This is one primary reason why the 2-minute rule is quite potent.

Examples of tasks you can turn into a 2-minutes project include:

- "Run three miles," is now "Tie my running shoes."

## Time Management

- "Fold the laundry" becomes "Fold one pair of socks."
- "Study for class" turns to "Open my notes."
- "Do 20 minutes of yoga" starts with "Take out my yoga mat."
- "Read before bed each night" becomes "Read one page."

You set the precedence to move onto more significant tasks by using the 2-minute rule to take immediate action on your goals.

## 5. Miscellaneous hacks

### 1. *When browsing with Google Chrome*

- **Pin websites to desktop**

If you visit some websites regularly, pin them to your desktop as apps. To do this, open the website you want to pin, go to Chrome settings, more tools, then, click on "create shortcut."

- **Use these popular Chrome shortcuts**
    - Ctrl+shift+n: opening a new window in incognito mode
    - Ctrl+j: open "recent downloads"
    - Shift+esc: Opens Google Chrome's task manager
    - Alt+enter: open URL in a new tab after typing the URL manually
    - Ctrl/shift+f5: reload the current page while ignoring cached content

### 2. *Do this last thing each night but the first thing each morning*

Send yourself an email before you sleep. This email should contain your top three goals for the next day. This is an often-overlooked productivity hack, yet it is straightforward.

Most times, you may have forgotten what you even wrote, probably because of stress, exhaustion, or a good night's sleep.

# Chapter 3 - A Guide to Goal-Setting

## All About the Goal-Setting Theory of Motivation

Edwin Locke proposed the goal-setting theory of motivation in the 1960s. This theory states that goal setting hugely depends on task performance. It says that specific, challenging goals with appropriate feedback results in higher and better task performance.

Goals indicate and guide the employee on the task to be achieved and the number of efforts required to accomplish it.

The efficiency of the goal depends on the type and quality of the goal.

Imagine you are 40 pounds overweight and need to drop the extra weight. Here are some options you have when setting the goal:

- "I want to shed the extra pounds before this time next year. I will review my diet and make appropriate recommendations." This goal isn't specific and lacks clarity. You need to specify the amount of weight you want to lose within that period and the particular steps to shedding this extra weight.
- "I will lose two pounds a week over the next four months. My exercise routine will be 40 minutes per day, five days a week. Also, I will include whole-grain products, vegetables, and three fruit servings in my diet. Lastly, I won't eat out at all for the next month. Then, I will only eat out once per week after the next month." This is a more specific and more clearly-defined goal than the previous one.

The principal motivation is the willingness to work towards achieving the set goal. Easy, general, and vague goals are less motivating than clear, specific, and challenging goals.

## Goal-Setting Principles

Based on his research in 1968, Dr. Edwin Locke published an article titled, *"Towards a theory of task motivation and incentives."* In this article, he provided proof that a clearly-defined goal with proper feedback motivates people to accomplish their goals. He also opined that the thrills involved in achieving a goal is a motivation in itself and improves performance. Summarily, Locke suggests that we tend to work harder to attain specific and challenging goals, especially in a work environment.

Years later, Dr. Gary Latham conducted his goal setting research in a work environment. Like Locke, he aimed to establish the correlation between setting goals and employee performance in the workplace.

In 1990, Locke and Latham jointly published their most famous work, *"A theory of goal setting & task performance."* The published work emphasized the importance of setting a specific and challenging goal. They also developed five basic principles responsible for success in goal setting.

Goals should:

- Be clear. A clearly-defined goal is more achievable than a poorly-defined one. Goals with a specific timeline of completion are usually the most effective.
- Be challenging. A goal with a slight level of difficulty will provide you with the motivation to accomplish the goal
- Involve a level of commitment. When you are committed to your goal, you will make the necessary effort to achieve the goal. Also, being accountable can increase your level of

commitment towards the goal. One simple and effective way to be responsible is to share your goal with a friend, relative, or trusted colleague.
- Have appropriate feedback. However, there has to be proper feedback to improve performance towards achieving the next goal. Feedback is the tool to regulate goal difficulties, make clarifications, and gain reputation. In a work environment, feedback helps the employee to be more involved in attaining the next goal. Hence, they become more satisfied with their job.
- Include the time for overcoming the learning curve. This is especially true for complex projects. Thus, having the time to master the learning curve gives you the best chance of success.

When employees are involved in setting the goal, they are more receptive towards the goal and are more involved in attaining the goal.

The goal-setting theory makes two specific assumptions:

**Assumption #1: Goal Commitment**

The goal-setting theory assumes that the individual will not abandon the goal because he's fully committed to it. However, you can only be committed to a goal when:

- It is open, accessible and the widespread
- You are not assigned the goal, but you are the one setting the goal
- Your set goal is consistent with your corporation; s goals and vision

**Assumption #2: Self-Efficiency**

This is your self-confidence and faith in performing the task. Your level of self-efficiency will determine the amount of effort you will apply when struggling with any aspect of the project. The reverse is also true; if your level of self-efficiency becomes too low, you may even quit before accomplishing the task.

## How to Apply the Goal-Setting Theory in Your Life

Carefully consider the goals you set when trying to improve an aspect of your daily life. Ensure that each task obeys the goal-setting principles discussed above.

Ensure you set goals that are suitable to one's abilities. For example, you could help your child succeed academically by allowing her to set the goal. For example, assume she wants to get 100% in her next English test. Not only is she committed to this goal, but the goal is also clear and challenging.

Now, you only need to discuss whether or not the goal is attainable. If she typically gets Cs in English assignments, it might be a poor goal to achieve a perfect score at the next attempt. Then, you need to develop specific steps towards achieving the goal. You also need to consider the amount of time required to achieve the objective and the complexity involved.

Ultimately, her goal might be: "I want a 100% score in my English test. I will start practicing neat and clean handwriting, then, learn how to use the appropriate words. My dad will give me feedback on how to fix my mistakes." Now, this is a specific plan to receive proper feedback because it is a clear, achievable goal, and she has the right motivation to achieve it. According to the goal-setting theory, she will perform better in her next test even if she couldn't obtain 100% on it.

The only limitation to the goal-setting theory is that it can fail when you lack the skill and competence to perform necessary actions towards achieving the goal.

Bear these principles in mind when next you want to determine your (individual or team) goals:

### 1. *Set clear and precise goals*

A clear goal is measurable and is devoid of understanding. The desired outcome will determine the explicitness of the objective and how it will be measured. Synonymous with the SMART goal-setting principle, clear goals should improve the understanding of the task, make results measurable and success inevitable. Consider how you will measure results. Does your goal excite you? Is it challenging enough? As you think about it, do you feel the motivation to complete it? If you answered negatively to any of these questions, you might have to reconsider this goal.

**Clear goal:**

- Implement technology to reduce product development time from 20 minutes to 15 minutes by the end of the year
- I want to lose 15 pounds in 2 months

**Unclear goal:**

- Decrease product development time
- I want to lose weight

When your goal is concrete and measurable, achieving it becomes easily possible, and you can easily track your progress.

### 2. *Make your goals challenging*

*"A goal that inspires your hopes, liberates your energy and commands your thoughts will make you happy."* - Andrew Carnegie.

To ensure you have the right degree of challenge, setting challenging goals requires a considerable balance. Your motivation and performance depend on the simplicity or difficulty in achieving the goal. You reach the highest level of motivation when your goal lies between difficult and easy.

The next time you set goals, make sure they are trying but attainable, challenging, but realistic. Here are a few questions you can ask yourself when setting your goals:

- Are they realistic and achievable?
- Do they provide enough motivation?
- Do they give enough challenge?

**Challenging:**

- Convert 65% more prospects to clients in Q3 FY 2018-19 compared with 45% Q2 FY 2018-19.
- Lose 40 pounds within two months

**Easily achievable:**

- Convert 1% more prospects to clients in Q3 FY 2018-19 compared to Q2 FY 2018-19.
- Lose 1 pound within two months

Your goal should be difficult enough to make you feel accomplished.

### 3. *Truly and genuinely commit to your goals*

You must fully understand and agree to your goals, whether you are setting the goal for yourself, your employees, or teammates before you can accomplish such goals. Mostly, when working in a team, your teammates will more likely work harder for the objective provided they have been involved in setting the goal. You shouldn't have any motivation problem till the goal is accomplished, provided the goal is achievable and consistent with the aspirations of all your teammates.

Imagine the tasks you accomplish daily at work; which ones do you exert the most effort and which ones do you perform without interest or enthusiasm. Your motivation to achieve your goals depends on your emotional commitment to the objective.

**Correct:** Project manager and his team decide the expected outcome of a meeting subject to each teammate's talent and skills.

**Incorrect:** Project manager does not consider his team's bandwidth and capabilities before assigning goals to each of them.

### 4. *Obtain feedback on your progress*

"Goal setting becomes hugely effective when you have feedback that shows progress relative to the intended goal" - Prof. Edwin Locke

Once you've chosen the right goal, you should obtain feedback to determine your level of progress. Thus, you can decide whether to adjust the goal or adjust your approach to attain the goal. Feedback can be self-adjudged, but it usually comes from other people.

**Correct:**

- Perform weekly checks on the design department to monitor their progress. Provide feedback on whether they need to alter the process, or they are on track.
- Tweak weight loss routine after losing one pound in two weeks

**Incorrect:**

- Set and forget about a task. When the deadline approaches, start getting anxious about completing the task.
- Wait after two months before tracking any changes

Frequently set aside some time to review your goals and track your progress. Thus, you are motivated continuously through the process of achieving your goal.

### 5. Simplify complex tasks

Be careful not to complicate your goals. When your objectives become too complicated, it negatively affects your motivation, productivity, and morale. Most people become overwhelmed when goals become highly complex. When you have complex goals, allow enough time to learn (when necessary), practice and improve performance until the goal is achieved. When necessary, modify the goal by reassessing its complexity or difficulty. You can also break those goals into smaller sub-goals.

Bear in mind that nothing worth its salt will ever be easily accomplished. But using simpler, less-complicated sub-tasks can help you to break down and overcome daunting tasks.

Remember that *"the journey of a thousand miles starts with taking the first step"* - Lao Tzu

**Correct:** Break down and distribute target sales among all salespeople, depending on their abilities. Thus, the entire target sales can be achieved within a specific period.

**Incorrect:** Expect one salesperson to achieve the entire target sales within a specific period

You need to keep working at your goal setting, just like every other aspect of your life. Use the principles to implement your life goals, and you will be surprised at the greatness you will achieve.

# 15 of the Best Tips for Effective Goal-Setting

You're virtually guaranteed success when you are clear about your life's purpose. You can determine your vision, convert your desires into achievable goals, and act on them.

My past experiences have taught me that being selective about my new year's goals, and thinking of ways to accomplish them has been hugely helpful. Goal setting is one proven way to transform impressive resolutions into actual results. Research shows that we are more likely to achieve our goals provided they are measurable.

When you have finished reading this section, you should have proven tips you can use to set your goals with greater efficiency:

1. **Make it physical.** Write down or type out your goals and action plans on paper. As you write them down, you will be more inclined to flesh them out. Thus, your action plans will not just be an outline. It will be a detailed roadmap you can follow.
2. **Regular review is key.** You should ensure that you review your goals at least once in a month, if not once a week. You can schedule an appointment with yourself, a team member, a trusted colleague, or relative for the review. Hence, you can track your level of progress easily. I review my yearly goals every week to ensure I'm on the right track of progress towards my goal.
3. **Challenge yourself without being stupid.** While it is good to choose goals that will excite and stretch you, you must also ensure that these goals are attainable. Thus, you can truly measure your progress over a specific period. The idea is to accomplish the goals and have something valuable you can celebrate at the end of the year. If you constantly have unachievable goals or white elephant projects, you start developing a habit of failure.
4. **Be exact with your action plans.** Write down the exact steps that can help you to accomplish your goal. For example, you need to show your business plan to potential investors when starting a business before they can take you seriously.
5. **Quality is always better than quantity.** Rather than having a long wish list of tasks which you may never

accomplish, why not have three or four solid goals? Once you've accomplished the most important goals, you can add more goals later.

6. **Be specific.** For example: create a blog with 10,000 monthly visitors is more specific than creating a blog with thousands of monthly visitors. Similarly, "gaining 1,500 Twitter followers" is more specific than "having a strong social media presence."

7. **Deadlines make concrete goals.** Your action plan is incomplete without a timeline to achieve the goal. Break down your big goal to smaller sub-goals. Then, set deadlines for these sub-goals till you attain the big goal.

8. **Accountability is important.** Share your goals with a friend or a loved one. They will make you accountable for achieving your goal. The law of commitment states that "When we tell others what we intend to accomplish, we have a natural tendency to remain committed till we achieve it." Thus, you have the needed impetus to take all the necessary steps until you can attain your goal.

9. **Make it obvious.** Tape your goals where they are pronounced. This place can be your door fridge or your bathroom mirror. If you stick it in a drawer, you will forget about it, and it won't do you any good. The idea here is to maintain top of mind awareness. You will easily forget what's not on top of your mind. Another way to keep your goals top of mind is to read your goals every day.

10. **Maintain flexibility.** When you have to scale back, recalibrate, or revise to take care of emergencies, ensure that these changes move you forward. This is one benefit of having a monthly review of your yearly goals.

11. **Love and appreciate the process.** The results you desire and the goal-setting process to achieve the goal are equally important. If you constantly think about what you're yet to

## Time Management

achieve, you won't appreciate the process or the sub-goals you've already achieved. When you appreciate and honor the adventure, you will remain positive, confident, and motivated.

12. **Use the rule of 5.** The rule of 5 ensures that you take daily steps towards attaining your goals. Identify and accomplish five specific steps that will get you closer to your goal. These steps don't have to be big. Sending an email or making a quick call is fine provided they are relevant to your goal. But quit for the day until you complete these five steps. Thus, you have a proven structure to maximize your day and give you a clarity of what you can achieve daily. If you use this rule and stick with it, you can make consistent progress without exhausting yourself. Where necessary, you can scale back your goals or round them up.

13. **Don't neglect self-care.** If you're malnourished, overworked, or stressed, you may never attain your goals. If you do, you may suffer ill-health as a result of the stress and overwork. While achieving your dreams, don't neglect self-care. Your body will thank you, and you will preserve your health and sanity.

14. **Keep score.** Why do you check the score immediately you tune into a sports station? You want to know which team is winning and how long for them to hold on. You should also be keeping score with the goals you've set. I suggest you use a physical chart. Identify the goal and outline the steps you need to achieve this goal. Track your progress and for every success, reward yourself. Using visual charts will show you that you are avoiding any shortcuts.

15. **Never give up.** If you don't give up but implement the tips above, you will succeed and achieve your goals even faster.

## 8 Common Reasons Why To-Do Lists Fail

Most people using to-do lists struggle to cross-out every item on the list by the time they are off to bed in the night. Even the tasks completed aren't part of the to-do lists. If to-do lists don't work for you, they would seem to be highly ineffective. You may be killing your productivity with your to-do lists. This section reveals why your to-do lists fail and what you can do about it.

### 1. You're allowing energy vampires

These are self-centered people who sap your energy without considering your time and priorities. They are the ones continually seeking your help over one task or the other. Most times, these are time-consuming tasks that are neither beneficial to you or on your to-do list.

If the energy vampire is a work colleague, you can send him this simple message. "I'm under a tight deadline now, and unfortunately, I can't help out at the moment." If this colleague remains persistent, send him a message similar to the one below: "I'm currently working on [state your current task here]. But I can loop in my supervisor and ask him how to prioritize."

### 2. You're writing your to-do list in the morning

Write your to-do list before going to bed. Thus, you avoid wasting your energized morning mojo to develop your daily tasks. A side benefit of creating your to-do list before going to bed is that it calms your mind. Psychiatrists and psychologists even recommend this technique to avoid anxiety. Keep out unwanted thoughts by establishing a plan for your next 24-hours. You won't disturb your sleep with thoughts of "you have a parent meeting at 2 pm" or "you must finish the report by 6 pm tomorrow."

### 3. Your to-do list has too many items

Out of 6,500 LinkedIn professionals, only 11% of them finish their to-do tasks by the end of the day. When you have too many items on your to-do list, you are setting yourself up for failure. Also, you deprive yourself of that end-of-day excitement of accomplishing your daily task. Also, when your to-do list is too much, it becomes highly discouraging. You will be more inclined to procrastinate since you won't know where to start.

Choosing at most three most important tasks is one effective way I've found to improve my productivity and manage my time correctly. Your most important tasks are measurable, generative, have meaning when completed, and move you towards accomplishing your goals.

### 4. You don't create time for urgent distractions

After making all the efforts to understand and write down your priorities. An email from a co-worker or a piece of breaking news is all it takes to distract you. So, you're off track the moment you receive your first urgent message despite all your productivity efforts.

A simple and effective solution is to create space in your schedule without any task. Thus, you have space to accommodate emergencies. Then, on days where there are no emergencies, you finish your day early and take the rest of the day off. You can also take proactive measures to avoid distractions. Adjust your email settings only to receive messages from specific people, set your phone calls to voicemails and make your status "busy" on private chats.

### 5. Your to-do list lack specificity

In an interview with Bloomberg Business, David Allen said, "Ninety-nine percent of every to-do list I have seen is an incomplete list of unclear stuff. You will see things like 'bank,' 'doctor,' or 'mom.' While these may look good, you need to include an action step with it." Instead of 'bank,' write down the specific task such as 'create a new savings account at the bank'."

## 6. You're not sorting your to-do list

After identifying your three most important tasks for the day, classify other goals into:

- A long-term list
- A weekly list.

Your long-term list should contain your 3-month or 6-month goal. For example, "completely cut out all unnecessary expenses." the weekly to-do list for this 6-month goal would be: "Stop eating out for the next X weeks."

## 7. Your to-do list lacks a deadline

There is no difference between a wish list and a to-do list without deadlines. Deadlines tilt us towards taking action. Where there are no deadlines, you lack the motivation to take action. This is one reason why your to-do list keeps growing without finishing most of the tasks on the list.

When you set deadlines, you prioritize tasks or projects to complete them within a specified timeframe. Remember Parkinson's law: *"Work expands to fill the time available for its completion."* You need to assign deadlines to your to-do items. Otherwise, don't be surprised that you can't finish most of the tasks.

## 8. You don't understand why you need a to-do list

For most people, when you ask them the basis for creating a to-do list, their answer is always: "to get things done." However, that's the wrong reason for creating a properly-designed to-do list. The primary purpose of a to-do list is to organize and highlight your most important tasks. By writing them down, you gain a panoramic view of your most essential duties.

A properly-designed to-do list should help you concentrate on the right work and avoid any distractions. Your task list is a tool to get the right things done; it's not a tool to get everything done. Reread the statement above again until you correctly understand the difference. When you misunderstand the role of your to-do list, you will create and use an ineffective one. Thus, rather than increase your productivity, you end up restricting it.

Now you have a to-do list approach that can make your day rather than break it. Note that you should write this long-term and weekly to-do list on a separate page in your journal.

# Chapter 4 - The Secrets of Productivity

## How to Prioritize When Everything Is Important

You're not alone; we all don't enough time to do everything we want to do. However, does everything on your to-do list feel important (or your superior feels that way)? Then, it's time for you to implement any of the prioritization techniques in this section. Thus, your to-do list can become more manageable and conquerable.

### What's a Prioritization Technique?

Which of the 150 tasks on your task list is the most important? The prioritization technique will help you to answer this question correctly. This technique provides you with a formal method to evaluate the importance of finishing each task on your list. By implementing the prioritization process, you can make the right decisions about the project you need to do. But delete the ones that are less urgent and less important. You can even specify a period for a particular task.

The prioritization techniques solve two vital issues:

**Issue #1:** Do you feel you've spent all your day performing urgent tasks for everyone who've sought your help? Then, a prioritized list will help you to avoid unreasonable last-minute panic assignments and regain control of your time.

**Issue #2:** Are those meeting requests or incoming emails that important? You'll never complete important work when you allow other people to create your to-do list for you through incoming emails and meeting requests. When you know the specific tasks to focus on and the reason to focus on that task, you can easily justify delaying answering that email or declining a meeting invite.

During my time in a product development team, we often use our prioritized list to prevent distractions and delays. When stakeholders made new and urgent requests, we show them the prioritized list. Then, ask, "Which task should we remove to accommodate your new request?" Often, once they see the importance of the other items on the list, their urgent requests suddenly become less urgent.

You can also use this technique to manage priorities with your family, co-workers, and your boss. It can also work for that part of your brain that's always searching for new ideas, giving you reasons to procrastinate on valuable work.

Use these prioritization techniques to focus on your most important work. You have to choose the right prioritization technique that makes sense and works for you. Fortunately, you can find a method that works for you from any of these prioritization techniques:

## 1. Priority Matrix

This technique involves distributing your tasks into a 4-box array. The y-axis represents a value, while the x-axis represents another one. Then, each quadrant represents a priority defined by the values.

The image below illustrated this technique.

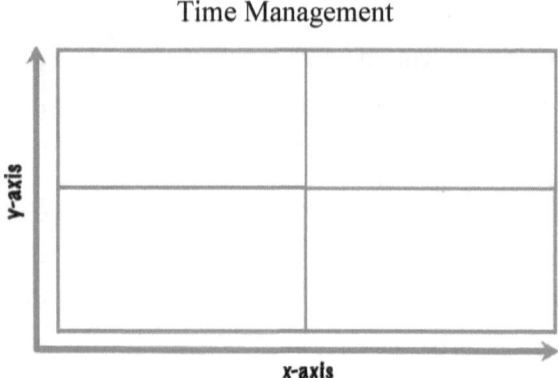

The Eisenhower matrix is a famous example of a priority matrix. In this matrix, urgency is the x-axis value, while importance is the y-axis value. Use urgency and importance to evaluate tasks, before placing each task in the correct quadrant. Thus, the Eisenhower matrix looks like the image below:

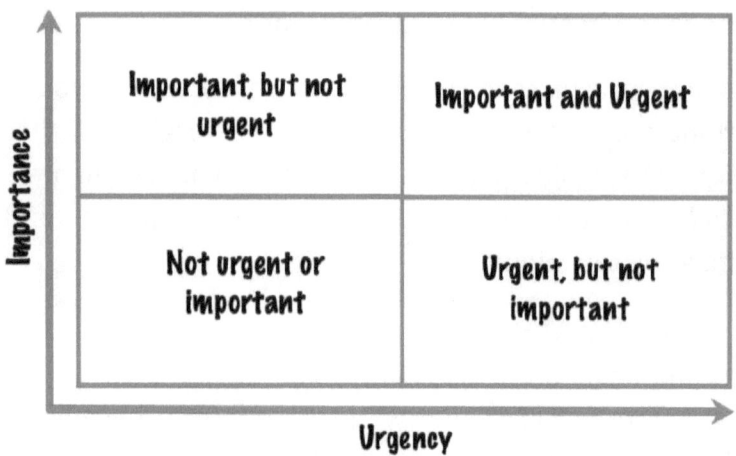

After placing each task in its suitable quadrant, you can determine what you need to delete from your list. You can also uncover what you need to delegate, what you need to work on later, and what you need to work on now.

Note that you can use any values that make sense to you as your x-and y-axis values in the priority matrix.

Here are two additional examples:

### a. *Effort-impact matrix*

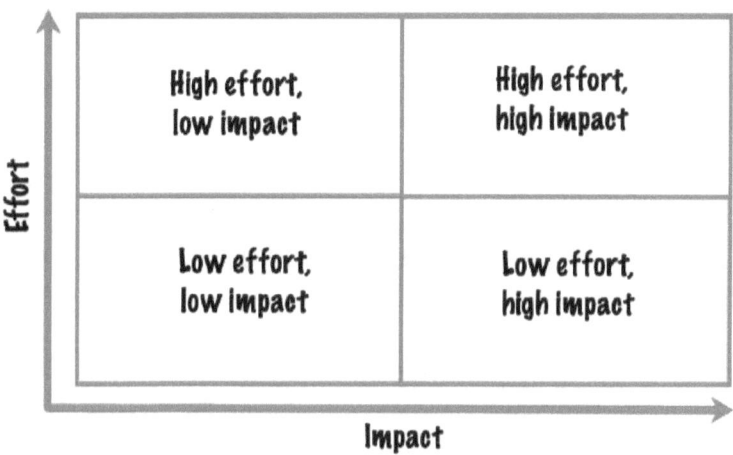

In this matrix, you assess tasks based on the effort you will exert to complete them and the impact of completing them. Your priorities are the tasks in the two right-side quadrants. Since the "low effort, high impact" tasks represent quick wins; they are likely your highest priorities.

### b. Value-cost matrix

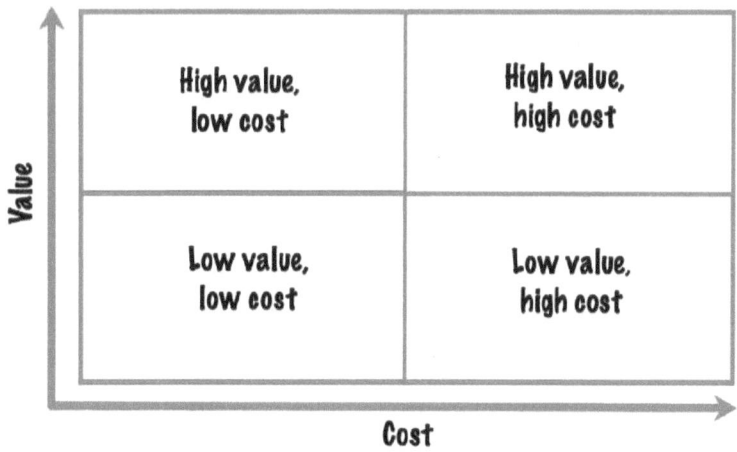

In this matrix, your priorities are the top two quadrants. Your quick wins are the "high value, low cost" tasks, but you should avoid executing "low value, high cost" tasks. If the priority matrix resonates with you, you can build your matrices in a spreadsheet, on paper, use the priority matrix app or the free Eisenhower matrix app.

## 2. MoSCoW (pronounced just like Russia's capital city)

In this simple prioritization technique, you categorize every task on your to-do list into four:

- M tasks-must do: Highly important tasks
- S tasks-should do: Though they are lower of a lower priority than m tasks, the s tasks are things you should do
- C tasks-could do: These are tasks you'd like to do. However, if you don't do them, it won't matter at all
- W tasks-won't do: These are tasks that aren't worth your time at all

**How to use this technique**

Use the MoSCoW to categorize each task. The order of priority of your tasks should be M, S, and C. Delete your W tasks.

Then, start working on your list from the top-down, and you can be sure that you're working on your highest-priority tasks.

Trello or any other Kanban app (available on Android and iTunes stores) is very useful for the MoSCoW method. Specify the order of each task by dragging and dropping them within the lists.

For optimal results with the MoSCoW method, ensure you add all your tasks to a master list before categorizing them. Use a zap (an automated Zapier workflow) to make this addition; it automates the movement of your mini-projects from Slack and your email inbox to your master to-do list.

## 3. ABCDE

A major demerit of the MoSCoW technique is that you can't use it for task delegation. The best alternative is to use Brian Tracy's ABCDE method (details in his "Eat The Frog" book). The ABCDE method is similar to the MoSCoW method.

- The A tasks are the M tasks in the MoSCoW method - do them
- The B tasks are the s tasks in the MoSCoW method
- The C tasks are the c tasks in the MoSCoW method
- The D tasks are tasks you should automate or delegate - this is the difference
- The E tasks are the w tasks in the MoSCoW method - delete them

Use the priority of each project to assign a letter to it. By delegating the D tasks and removing the E tasks, you can focus on the A, B, and C tasks - the most critical tasks.

You can also use Kanban apps for this technique. Your master list should sub-lists with A, B, C, D, and E tasks. Drag and drop tasks into the right category from the master list, then, start with your A tasks.

## 4. Agile Prioritization

This prioritization method, also known as scrum prioritization, relies on ordering your tasks. If you have 15 to-dos on your task list, use priority and sequence to arrange the mini-projects from 1-15. Scrum prioritization is highly effective when the series is highly essential. For example, assuming your most important task is to retile your bathroom floor, but they also have to run new pipes. Though running new pipes is a lower priority, it needs to be completed first because it will affect your most important task: retiling the floor.

There are three criteria for evaluating task in scrum prioritization:

- The importance of the project
- The significance of the project relative to other tasks
- Other projects that can affect this task

Assign each of these criteria a number 1 to N (N = total number of items on your list). Every item should have a unique number. No two tasks can be #1. Though scrum prioritization can be combined with the MoSCoW and ABCDE techniques, it's also useful on its own. Consider the inter-dependence of the tasks on one another before categorizing them by priority. Then, arrange them in order of completion.

Any drag-and-drop to-do list app is suitable for scrum prioritization. But for efficiency, rather than using drag and drop tools, you can use Yodiz (a scrum-specific tool) to assign numbers to each task. Yodiz has a free plan.

## 5. Bubble Sort

Let's rephrase criteria #2 of the scrum prioritization technique to "how important is a task relative to other tasks?" The bubble sort is a technique that compares the importance of tasks relative to one another. Hence, it's a useful technique for answering the question above. The first step to using this technique is to arrange all your to-do items on a horizontal grid:

| Task 1 | Task 2 | Task 3 | Task 4 | Task 5 | Task 6 |
|--------|--------|--------|--------|--------|--------|

Your next step is to compare the first two tasks and identify the most important one. Then, move the most critical item to the top left. Using the image above, assuming task 2 is more important than item 1, then, it becomes the first task of the horizontal grid.

Continue to compare the two closest tasks until you exhaust the list of tasks using the question above as the basis for rearranging the order of items.

After reordering the list completely, your least important priority is now to the far right, while your most important priority is now on the far left.

An example of a completely reordered list in order of priority is shown below:

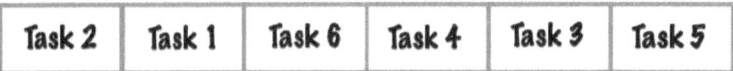

Though there are no specific tools suitable for this technique, any project management app appropriate for drag-and-drop prioritization can work effectively. But instead of working on tasks from left-to-right, you work on them from top-to-bottom.

## 6. The 1-3-9 Technique

This technique allows you to prioritize urgent but less important tasks. Each day you are to complete 13 tasks:

- Nine low-importance items
- Three somewhat important tasks
- One crucial task

First, work and complete your one tasks, then, your three tasks and lastly, your nine tasks. The 1-3-9 method helps you to work on the most important of your less important tasks.

## 7. Two Lists

This technique is credited to Warren Buffet. Here's how it works: write down 25 to-do tasks, then, circle the top five items on this list. Next, group these tasks into two extensive lists. The first list which contains the five tasks you circled is now your to-do list. The second list which includes the other 20 items is now your don't do list. Complete all your five to-do tasks before spending any time on your don't do list. While you could accomplish this technique with any app that allows you to move tasks between lists, it is a technique designed to be performed on paper.

## How to Choose Your Most Suitable Prioritization Technique

The goal of these prioritization techniques is the same - to help you work on your highest priority tasks. Hence, it doesn't matter whether you use one technique, multiple techniques, or combine parts of the different techniques. You must ensure that the technique you choose makes sense, feels natural, and is adequate for you.

## The Chunking Technique for Making Your Goals Achievable

These days, we are pulled in a lot of directions on our personal and professional lives that the idea of free becomes an illusion. But imagine:

- You can bring higher efficiency to your life
- You can focus on achieving your goals rather than trying to accomplish an infinite number of tasks on your to-do lists

Imagine the free time it will open in your life and the positive change in the quality of your life. This desire to create free time is the basis of the rapid planning method (RPM). Apart from being a time management system, RPM helps you to focus on critical aspects that can help you to organize your life more efficiently. Thus, you can maximize your sense of fulfillment, joy, and optimize your desired outcomes. The assumption is that you are more driven to take actions that lead to your success when you have a clarity of purpose that drives your actions. Chunking (a highly efficient way to maximize your day) is one of the core components of RPM.

## What is Chunking?

Chunking means arranging information into bit-sized pieces to produce your desired outcome without shutdown or stress. One source of stress in our lives is that we don't have enough time to do an infinite number of things for our lives. This strong emotion to get things done leads to the creation of to-do lists. But a large number of items on the list can lead to frustration. Thus, we won't even tackle any project on our list.

Based on my experience, three chunking methods have been the most effective:

- Chunk down by quantity
- Chunk down by the time
- Chunk down by actionable steps

### 1. *Chunk down by quantity*

This means setting a quota. If you are a writer, you can set a quota for your writing. For example, you can write a maximum of 3 pages per day until you complete your novel.

Alternatively, your quota can be a word count. An example is a national novel writing month challenge. If you are a participant, you will be required to write 1,667 words per day, and by the end of the month, you would have completed a 50,000-word book.

Here are three other examples of chunking down a goal by quantity:

- Hit 300 balls daily to improve your tennis
- Learn ten French words per day for 100 days to improve your French fluency
- Do one drawing per day for one year to improve your drawing fluency

## 2. *Chunk down by the time*

A while back, I was overweight because I was making bad food choices, eating out a lot, and wasn't exercising. After choosing to shed some pounds, my nutritionist and I developed a plan for me to lose 30 pounds in three months. He provided me with a menu of what to eat during this month. I was also instructed to walk one hour daily.

Walking one hour per day became a significant component of chunking down my goal. Thus, I used the time to chunk down my goal of losing weight.

Here are some other goals that can be chunked down by time:

- Declutter for 10 minutes daily to be organized
- Practice piano for 40 minutes daily to become a master pianist
- Meditate for 15 minutes daily to manage stress

However, spending an hour per day to achieve my important goals remains my favorite way of chunking down my goals.

### 3. Chunk down by actionable steps

By creating a list of actionable steps, you can chunk down a goal you are not sure you could achieve. Goal, sub-goals, and actionable steps are three terms we would use to describe this method.

By definition,

- The goals are the target you intend to achieve
- Sub-goals are the milestones to achieve the goals
- Actionable steps are the single tasks to accomplish each sub-goal

Assuming you intend to "create a video course," but you've never created a course or made videos. Your first step is to establish a deadline for the video course creation. Let's use a 6-month (180-day) deadline. Next, open excel and create 180 spaces (a space for each day); this is your actionable steps list.

Now, create ten sub-goals to achieve your big goal. Anytime you need help with any creating the sub-goals, you can:

- talk to a video course creation expert,
- read a book about it,
- watch some YouTube videos, or perform online research.

For our video course creation example, here are ten sub-goals to achieve this goal:

- Suitable equipment
- Learning how to use the equipment
- Developing the title for the course
- Validate your title idea
- Develop your outline
- Develop the script
- Design the slides
- Start recording the videos
- Edit your videos (I recommend you outsource)

- Launch your course

To make things easy, let's assume each sub-goal has a deadline of 18 days (i.e., 180 days (the total deadline) divided by 10 (the number of sub-goals)). Thus, we need 18 actionable steps to achieve each sub-goal.

You can use the following guideline to create your actionable steps.

Actionable step for each day:

- One - what you can do right away to get started
- Two - the next physical action to take
- Repeat the steps above till you have actionable steps to complete your first sub-goal

If you complete a sub-goal in less 18 days, move to the next sub-goal. Then, continue until you accomplish your goal. As write down actionable steps, ask yourself this question: "Am I capable of taking the step immediately?" If your answer is "yes," then include this actionable step. Otherwise, break down this step further.

You can also use the CRUMBB technique, an acronym for "clearly realizable unit that's a meaningful building block." Realizable means you can take action immediately, while Meaningful means it moves you closer to complete your goal. You can read more about the CRUMBB method in a book titled "master the moment" written by best-selling author, Pat Brans.

Use any of the three methods to chunk down your goals. By breaking down your goals and tackling them in bite-sized pieces, you can easily save time and achieve your goals.

# 5 of the Biggest Productivity Killers and How to Overcome Them

We all aspire to become good time managers and achieve high levels of productivity. However, we experience several obstacles and distractions hinder us from achieving the goals before we can even think of surpassing such goals.

In this section of the chapter, you will discover severe time-wasters and top productivity killers.

### 1. Busyness

Activities in this category include calling unnecessary meetings, making unnecessary phone calls, organizing email, and cleaning the desk. Most people indulge in excess busywork for the sake of being busy. When you indulge in these non-substantial activities, you are not productive.

How to overcome: set aside one hour per day to delegate all these tasks. Then, you can easily focus on your high priority list of items.

### 2. Excessive planning

With planning, you are sure you won't miss any important thing. You already know your next actions, and you can focus on your goals with your task list. However, rather than do any actual work, it's much easier to spend time to update and organize your calendar.

How to overcome: set aside one day in 21 days to review undone tasks. Also, spend 15 minutes each morning to review your previous day's performance and update your goals for the day. Evernote and Day One apps are quite useful for this purpose.

### 3. Less sleep

One of the biggest productivity killers is sleeping less and staying up late. When you sleep less, you do things slowly because it is tough for you to get moving. Hence, you become addicted to coffee before you can have a productive day.

While it may not be necessary to get a full eight hours of sleep, ensure you get enough sleep that makes you productive for the day. Thus, you avoid relying on chemicals which can pose a severe health issue in the nearest future.

## 4. Email inbox

Email is highly addictive, and it is the biggest time sucker in business or personal life. Worse, you won't get any work done. When you email a client or colleague, and you discuss work, you are not dealing with your problems but helping others solve their problem.

**3 simple and effective ways to overcome email overwhelm:**

1. Check your email three times per day. This can be an hour before you get to work, after lunch, and just before you sleep. Thus, you can be sure you're not missing out anything.
2. Use Boomerang for Gmail to schedule replies and set up reminders to follow up on sent emails. Thus, you are in control of your time because you can send all your replies at once.
3. Don't write more than a paragraph of response to your email. A better and more effective option is to make a quick call, then, write a short email to act as the paper trail.

When I implemented this technique, I spend less than an hour on emails instead of two hours. I tracked my time using RescueTime,

## 5. Multitasking

Multitasking means switching between tasks constantly. As humans, our brains can't handle several complex tasks simultaneously. When you multitask, you are unproductive because you produce less quality work, make more mistakes and sometimes, lose more money.

**How to overcome**: Reread the previous sections in this chapter.

# Chapter 5 - Dealing with Distractions

## The Difference Between Internal and External Distractions

Before differentiating between internal and external distractions, here's an explanation about each of them.

### Internal Distractions

Internal distractions are generated from our self-image and perceptions; they come from our inside. You are experiencing internal distractions each time your plan for a day is delayed or hindered by your thoughts or self-perceptions. Unruly negative ego (especially, lack of self-acceptance, lack of self-love, or both) is usually the primary cause of internal distractions. It involves your desire to be in control to change others or make specific changes about yourself. These thoughts eventually become a self-imposed internal struggle, which leads to frustration.

Compared to internal distractions, it is easier to overcome external distractions. You need to be in control of your mind to overcome internal distractions. That is, you must be mentally disciplined. When you have lots of things on your mind, you will be less productive. For example, you will struggle to focus when you have a health issue, are dehydrated or haven't gotten enough sleep. Also, if you are experiencing some challenges in your relationship, you will struggle to focus.

More importantly, internal distractions prevent you from doing actual work. When you don't have a real purpose or mission, you do nothing. If you don't spend sufficient time to consider your real goals (whether long-term or short-term goals), you won't do anything. You must spend the time to plan your week and days, then, commit to doing what moves you closer to your goals.

Thus, you will avoid sitting in a reactive mode, waiting for someone to provide you with what to come or for the world to work for you. Thus, you can manage your time properly and be truly productive. When you experience internal distractions (which is bound to happen), you must leave them for their proper time. Otherwise, you won't focus on being productive with your time.

## External Distractions

There are a lot of external distractions that can affect your focus negatively. You need to pay attention to some of these distractions because they are vital.

Examples;

- Your child needs a ride home because she called in sick from school.
- Your best client needs your attention because he's struggling with a severe challenge

While these external distractions can and does happen, they are not frequent enough to affect your productivity. However, most external distractions shouldn't command your attention because they aren't that important. Examples of unimportant external distractions include countless novelties and trivialities on the internet or conversation about the walking dead, game of thrones or any other popular television shows.

Generally, everything else that you can use as an excuse not to plan or execute your plan is an external distraction.

If you are disciplined and thoughtful enough, you can shut down, turn off, and avoid external distractions.

You will discover proven ways to eliminate external distractions later in this chapter.

## Types of Internal Distractions

In this section, you will discover the types of internal distractions that exist. The usual emphasis is on eliminating distractions, but you need to know the types of internal distractions before you can prevent or get rid of them. Knowing the types will help you to realize your kind of inner distraction and the best way to eliminate it.

### Type 1: Self-doubt

Insecurity (and not lack of talent) is the biggest killer of dreams. You can turn your self-doubt to a self-fulfilling prophecy when you believe things such as:

"I can't compete with other businesses" or

"I'll never get promoted."

Regardless of your confidence, there are times you are going to experience a little self-doubt. It happens to all of us. However, you must be mentally healthy to prevent self-doubt so that you can achieve your goals.

Self-doubt makes you lose your self-confidence. Self-doubt can make you quit before reaching your goal. This is a significant distraction. Boosting your self-esteem is the best way to get rid of this inner distraction. A few ways you can improve your self-confidence are:

# Time Management

### 1. Staying focused on the present

For example, you are running out into an athletic field or on a stage, but within you, you're thinking, "I will embarrass myself." This thought will affect your performance negatively. Instead of allowing your inner monologue to pull you down, focus on the present. Remind yourself that you don't need to strive for perfection; you only need to do your best. Thus, you can pour in all your energy to achieve better performance.

### 2. Control your emotions

Your thoughts and actions are highly dependent on your emotions. Unless you take proactive measures to control your emotions, anxious feelings can trigger doubtful thoughts and mar your performance.

Monitor the influence of your emotions on your choices. Control your anxiety and calm your mind by distracting yourself with mundane tasks, going for a walk, or taking deep breaths. Don't cave in, give up, or bail out on account of your short-term discomfort.

### 3. Ask yourself, "What's the worst thing that can happen?"

Wild predictions such as "I'm going to mess up everything" can lead to self-doubt. When these doubtful thoughts start creeping in, consider the worst-case scenario. Should you make a mistake, how bad would be the consequences of your error? The truth is, any mistake is not likely to be life-altering. Failing to get a promotion, stumbling over your lines or losing a game won't be that relevant in a few years. So, calm your nerves by keeping things in proper perspective.

### 4. *Consider the evidence supports your distracting thoughts*

Ask yourself, "What's the proof that I can't or can do this?" Your answer to this question will give you a realistic perspective. Though this technique won't eliminate all your self-doubt, it will reduce it significantly.

### 5. *Don't worry about a little self-doubt*

According to a 2010 study published in the Psychology of Sport And Exercise, slight insecurity can lead to better performance. When you're aware that things might not go according to plan, create a few minutes to plan how you can improve. This few minutes of planning will help you, in the long run, to utilize your time correctly. Self-confidence remains the best way to eliminate self-distractions.

## Type 2: Overthinking and distressful thoughts

If you're fretting about how you will succeed tomorrow or beating up yourself over a mistake you made yesterday. Then, you are suffering from distressful thoughts. Thus, you are in a constant state of anguish, and you are unable to get out of your head.

Though we all over-think things now and then, it shouldn't be too constant. Two of the destructive thought patterns in this internal monologue are worrying and ruminating.

Ruminating involves going over previous actions. Examples of ruminating thoughts include:

- I spoke up too soon at the meeting today. I could tell from their eyes that they thought I was an idiot.
- I was stupid to have left my old job. If I had stayed, I would have been happier.
- My parents were right. I won't amount to anything.

Worrying involves negative predictions about your future. Examples include:

- My presentation tomorrow will be embarrassing. Everyone will conclude that I'm not competent because my hands will be shaking and my face will turn red throughout the presentation.
- It doesn't matter what I do; my promotion will never happen.
- I'm no longer good enough for my spouse. He/she will divorce me and find someone else.
- I should help Edward with his task and destroy my time management plan for the day because Edward helped during my previous task.

Sometimes, distressful thoughts can be in the form of negative imaginations such as imagining your car veering off the road. Overthinking everything prevents you from taking any productive activity.

### *Effects of overthinking*

Overthinking can have a severe negative impact on your well-being.

Evidence from an NCBI research suggests that you are more susceptible to mental health problems when you dwell on your problems, mistakes, or shortcomings. Your tendency to ruminate increases as your mental health declines, leading to a vicious cycle that you may never break.

Another study also showed that severe emotional distress could be the result of overthinking. When you can't sleep even after shutting your mind, then, you know you are an overthinker. With fewer hours of sleep and more reduced sleep quality, your time management for the next day will completely poor because you will desire more rest.

## Type 3: Shiny object syndrome

Shiny object syndrome involves distraction through new products, tools, and ideas. These 'bright shiny objects' seem more fun and more exciting than your current projects. Sometimes, you may even think this new project has more prospects than the project you are working on at the moment.

If you can relate to any of the following, then, you are suffering from shiny object syndrome:

- Rather than complete what you are currently doing, you continuously jump from one goal to another
- You are fascinated by the wild claims of various e-courses. Thus, you jump to another e-course without implementing what you learn from the previous one.
- Instead of executing one of your business ideas, you keep compiling a list of business ideas.
- Rather than build the basics, you spend too much time on new ideas and tools, 95% of which is noise.

One of the best ways to overcome shiny object syndrome is getting into the habit of completing a task before moving to the next one. In the next section of this chapter, you will discover proven ways to silence internal distractions.

# 13 Ways to Silence Internal Distractions

In the previous section, we discussed the types of internal distractions, but we didn't discuss how to stop them except for the first type of distraction. In this section, you will discover how to silence types two and three internal distractions. Also, you will find other ways to silence internal distractions.

# 4 Ways to Stop Overthinking

You can limit your negative thinking patterns with consistent practice. Here are the six proven ways to stop overthinking:

### 1. *Start paying attention to the way you think*

The first step to putting an end to overthinking is awareness. When you observe that you're replaying events in your mind repeatedly, bring yourself to the conscious fact that your thoughts can't change the past.

### 2. *Learn to recognize and replace thinking errors*

Since negative thoughts can be highly exaggerated, you must acknowledge and replace them with positive thoughts. Otherwise, you may erroneously assume that you will be fired for calling in sick or that you will become homeless because you forget a deadline.

### 3. *Focus on solving the problem*

Looking for solutions is more helpful than dwelling on your problems. Deduce lessons from a mistake or develop steps to prevent a future issue. Always ask yourself, what can I do about it? Rather than asking, why did this happen?

### 4. *Create time to reflect*

A little time of reflection can help you to manage your time for the rest of the day properly. Through your meditation, you should identify possible holes in your plan or what you could differently to be successful. Your daily schedule should include 20 minutes of thinking time. Allow your mind to wander excessively during this time. Then, when the 20 minutes is up, move into productive tasks. When you observe that you've started overthinking outside your thinking time, remind yourself that you will think about it later. You may have to repeat this reminder more than once before it becomes effective.

## 5 Tips to Overcome Shiny Object Syndrome

It is when you are focused that you can manage your time satisfactorily and get things done. But you need to avoid shiny object syndrome before you can become entirely focused. Here are five proven tips to overcome shiny object syndrome:

1. **Learn to differentiate between real opportunities and shiny objects**

Shiny objects are actual distractions that disguise as excellent and exciting tools. For example, some new tools are being introduced into the market that makes a lot of bold claims. But won't add value to your productive work or life. Real opportunities must have an actual impact on your life or work. For example, tools that improve your product or service delivery and tools that can boost your workflow.

2. **Use the "wait and see" technique**

Use this technique when you're unsure about your next decision. Many tools are fast becoming obsolete within a couple of years due to rapid technological advancements. If new software is introduced into the market and claiming to make you more productive, critically analyze whether or not you need that tool. You should only buy this new tool when you are sure that you have no alternative.

3. **Remove low-quality information sources**

Managing sources of distraction is one of the best ways to manage distraction. When you subscribe to newsletters that recommend new products frequently, you will always struggle to focus because you want to assess each product before making a purchase decision. This is called cognitive load. Your best option is to remove low-quality information sources rather than using your precious mental energy to sieve out the noise. Evaluate your email subscriptions, Facebook group memberships, and social media news feeds. Unsubscribe from groups and newsletters that offer unhelpful, irrelevant suggestions.

### 4. Don't follow the bandwagon

Assess the suitability of a new tool for your work and life before buying it. Don't buy it or use it because your colleagues are calling it the best thing to happen since sliced bread. This new tool can become your source of unproductivity. Always ask yourself these three critical questions:

- What are the merits vs. demerits of doing this?
- What value will this add to my life or work?
- Do I need it?

If you are genuinely sure that it will add value to your work and life, then, do it.

### 5. Don't waste your time chasing trends

If you continuously follow every new tool and idea, you won't get things done. You will only be wasting your time chasing trends. Also, understand that a new product doesn't mean it's a better product.

## 4 Other Ways to Overcome Internal Distractions

Now, here are four other ways to silence any form of internal distractions:

### 1. Practice cognitive defusion

Most of our intrusive thoughts are rhetorical and abstract. One effective way to lose the power of your negative thoughts is to reframe those thoughts until they lose their meaning. Cognitive defusion is a technique that changes a word or phrase and how it impacts you. For example, if you always repeat a phrase such as "life is meaningless," you can reframe it to "I'm having a thought that life is meaningless." Repeating the reframed sentence removes any negativity out of it. Similarly, if you hear a word in your head repeatedly when you feel inadequate ('loser') or mess up ('stupid'), saying it out repeatedly dilutes its power. The key is to verbalize the thought so that you can hear it.

A similar technique to cognitive defusion is called the positive effect or positive direction. As the name suggests, this technique involves reframing negative words into positive words. You can turn words such as "I can't do this" into "Of course, I can be successful." "I will never achieve this goal" becomes "I'm definitely going to make this happen." When you use such positive phrasing, you prime your frontal lobes and consequently, stimulate a goal-directed behavior.

## 2. *Practice self-compassion*

Self-compassion is the act of treating yourself with kindness. You use a gentle understanding and soothing to respond to your anxiety. When you start having anxious thoughts such as "Oh no, here we go. I can't take this. I hate these thoughts."

Self-compassion can turn this internal dialogue to "It's not easy to feel this way, but you can overcome these problems and complete the task." This technique lessens the effects of the anxiety by encouraging you not to blame yourself for feeling anxious. It helps you to approach the fear from a place of understanding.

## 3. *Verbalize your thoughts*

Since what's floating in your head is often a bunch of unordered thoughts and worries, talking in your head rarely reveals anything significant. However, when you verbalize your feelings and fears, you can develop a story and identify the meaning of the story. If you don't like to a person, journal it. The effects are similar.

Writing helps with physical and psychological issues since it leads to the development of a coherent narrative over time. It is the cognitive processing during writing that makes it a therapeutic activity. By creating a description, you can have an idea of what's happening. Hence, reducing part of those awful cycle of mind chatter.

Another writing technique is to write out the tasks you want to achieve within the next hour. Then, set a deadline for you to finish the tasks. The act of writing out your critical hourly tasks will refocus your brain on your most vital projects. Adding a deadline creates a sense of urgency that helps you to remain focused.

### 4. Practice mindfulness and meditation

If you're stuck in your head and need a quick grounding in the present, mindfulness can be more accessible. It is slightly different from meditation. The best description of mindfulness is by Jon Kabat-Zinn, *"Focus on the present moment on purpose without being judgmental."*

At every moment, always refocus your attention on what you're doing at that moment. Take a moment to focus on the present instead of what's in your head. Thus, you can snap yourself out of your internal distractions when it happens.

# 6 Reliable Ways to Defeat External Distractions

External distractions usually derails our daily work ethic. This can be anything from your neighbor's little child running past your office window, an unexpected knock on the front door, or a colleague stopping by for a chat. You could be distracted by notifications from Skype, social media newsfeeds, or email.

Most times, we are at fault for these distractions. Most of us are guilty of checking Facebook newsfeeds or email when we should be doing actual work. At other times, distractions happen just like life happens. Hence, you must regain your concentration instantly to prevent the busyness from consuming your minds.

Since prevention is better than cure, you must find proven ways to minimize these distractions. When our attempts to prevent distractions fail, it's crucial that you have strategies in place to deal with them. Here are six reliable ways of defeating external distractions:

### 1. *Attention firewalling*

In recent years, famous figures such as Merlin Mann, Gina Trapani, and Tim Ferriss have made this concept popular in productivity circles. This technique involves preventing distractions rather than dealing with it.

You must track your activities and identify the distractions that prevent you from doing productive work. For instance, you can use software to block access to a specific website that wastes too much of your time. If it remains a distraction because you could bypass the software. You can prevent it by using your router. Since you will need to reset the router and save the change, it would be a bit harder to bypass the router. During that time, you won't be distracted by the internet, and you have a high probability of focusing and refocusing on your tasks when you are distracted.

For email, uninstall notifiers and change the settings of your phone to silent to avoid the beeping sounds of new messages.

## 2. *Keep your to-do list readily visible*

Keeping your to-do list nearby makes it easier to get back on task during your waiting period and keep your focus clear. Hence, you can avoid falling into the distraction trap. Also, ensure you write your to-do list legible such that you can read it from your most common working position.

Set up little reminder messages such as "are you on task?" to help you regain focus during times you start wandering. The real secret is to make your task list visible all the time and be mindful of it.

## 3. *Keep a procrastination pad.*

This procrastination pad can be by your desk or on your computer. Jot notes about your distractions in them as they come. Thus, you can forget about them and come back to them later. An alternative is to use a separate device to store your distractions. For example, you can have a jotter titled "procrastination pad," which contains your distractions.

## 4. *Maximize your productivity peaks*

We all have specific periods of the day where we are at peak productivity. You need to identify these times and give yourself the best advantage by scheduling your most important for these times.

## 5. *Psyche yourself up to work*

A compelling reason to complete work is highly essential in staying on task. Remind yourself about the benefits of finishing your task. For example, a work-free weekend or the pride in finishing a challenging project. Reminding yourself of some short-term benefits also works. For example, if you complete a specific amount of work, you can have enough time to rest and take your wife on a date for the night.

### 6. *Use the instant-reward technique*

Tell yourself you would do something entertaining for 10 minutes once you can complete your next task within a specific timeframe. For example, if you complete 600 words of an article within the next 30 minutes, you will play your favorite game on your phone for 5 minutes. If your work allows you to work remotely, you can use this technique to sharpen your focus. However, this method should be your last resort because it's almost impossible to do your best work within 20- or 30-minute timeframes. It's a good strategy when you are too distracted or when you struggle to start your day with productive work.

# Chapter 6 - Emulating Success

## Goal Setting Examples from The Business Masters

In this section, we explore the goal-setting secrets of some great business executives. Let's get started:

### 1. Barbara Corcoran

Barbara is a "Shark Tank" investor and founder of Barbara Corcoran Inc.

*"Due to time constraints, I usually organize my list in sections. The first section is for calls I intend to make, but it doesn't exceed three calls. I put my calls into the first section to avoid forgetting about them.*

*The review section is my second section. These are typically short tasks. In it, I answer questions such as 'Would you like to be on our show?' I can do a quick review and get it out of the way since the relevant paperwork is attached to it. Though they are not listed in any particular order, I ensure I complete them in less than a day.*

*The third section is my project list. These contain tasks that move my business forward and make me money. I further categorize them as A, B, and C, depending on importance. Some of the tasks in this list are companies I've invested in through* Shark Tank. *The A tasks are essential and today-only. The B tasks are also necessary, but their deadline is not today.*

*When my task list is too small, it shows that I haven't created time for reflection. My list grows more substantial when I have more time to reflect. When I reflect, I'm able to think of new opportunities that I don't want to forget. Despite trying various to-do lists, my useful to-do lists have been the ones typed or written. There is a satisfaction that I get with crossing off tasks that I can't get with using the delete button."*

## 2. Jim McCann

Jim is the author of *Talk is (Not) Cheap: The Art of Conversation Leadership* and the founder and CEO of 1-800-flowers.com, Inc.

*"I've been using lists for most parts of my business life. I had a crazy list-maker as a mentor at St. John's home in Queens, New York. Being busy is easy, but being effective is a lot harder. Using my mentor's example, I bought a pad and printed 'things I have to do today' on it. Currently, I combine physical and digital pads. My list is divided into four:*

- *Things I must do today*
- *A general to-do list*
- *A projects list*
- *A long-term ideas list. These are highly important for the company's growth.*

*Before assigning my jottings to any of the lists above, I ask myself one question: 'Must it be done today?' Most of these jottings are useful ideas that fit for the long-term ideas list or the projects list. My team assesses these lists from time to time to determine whether or not the ideas are still good enough for implementation. We replace the ideas that are no longer good enough with new ones. With a proper task list, you can become a better manager of your time."*

## 3. Jim Koch

Jim Koch is the founder of the Boston Beer Company.

*"Priority tasks from different internal teams determine my day. Every morning, I write down a maximum of five must-do goals for that day on a Post-it note. This act keeps me focused for the day.*

*While these items not necessarily urgent, they are important. Once I start my day, I ensure that the list remains reachable to avoid procrastinating on them. However, I strike out all items on the list by the close of each day. Also, each of my weeks starts with a maximum of five emails in my inbox. To ensure that issues or questions are resolved pretty quickly, I respond to emails almost immediately after I receive them. Thus, responding to emails doesn't affect my productivity during my daily breaks.*

*During my break-time, I switch off my internet and spend that time at the nearest hardware store. I may even pick up a tool I need at home. By the time I return to my desk, I will make headway with my previous issue or dilemma."*

## 4. Daymond John

Daymond is the founder of the famous clothing line, FUBU, and he is the author of the *Power of Broke.*

*"I have a set of 10 goals. The first seven goals are 6-month goals. The rest are 5-year, 10-year, and 20-year goals. Since I want my goals to be the last thing I think and dream about, I make it a habit to read my goals every morning and every night. I write down the seven goals on a piece of paper. While each goal has an expiry date, I include a few details of how I will achieve each goal. The first five goals are health, family, business, relationship, and philanthropy goals. The next two are personal financial goals and business project goals. Each goal is written in a positive language. For example, if my goal is to reduce my weight to 170 pounds by July 5. The few details would be to eat fish, drink eight glasses of water daily, and exercise twice per day. It won't include avoiding alcohol, meat, and fried foods."*

## 5. Yunha Kim

Yunha is the founder and CEO of Simple Habit, a meditation app.

*"Setting time limits is one of my workflow secrets. We often have never-ending lists of to-dos at a startup like ours. Hence, it is not feasible to fully finish a task in one sitting."*

# 13 Time Management Hacks of Successful People

It is not easy to manage or maximize your time. But by knowing the tips and tricks of today's most successful people, you can use their tips or develop your time management strategies. Thus, improving your productivity. Learn more about various unconventional time-saving tricks from the time management tricks of some of the world's most successful people.

## 1. Sir Richard Branson delegates emails

Sir Richard is the founder of the Virgin group. He is also a British business magnate, investor, author, and philanthropist.

*"I check reader emails in the morning. I pass some to colleagues, dictate the ones with quick answers to my assistants. But I write the more detailed responses personally. I check my email in bursts to focus on my current tasks. I give my employees space rather than directives. I am comfortable allowing them to take responsibility because I hired people I trust."*

## 2. Jack Dorsey creates daily themes

Jack is the CEO and co-founder of payment processing experts, Square and social media company, Twitter. Dorsey runs these two significant companies simultaneously by giving each day a theme. Dorsey spends each day of the week to focus on a particular primary area. For example, Mondays can be for product development, and Tuesdays can be for general management functions. Wednesdays can be buffer days where you respond to low-priority emails and tasks.

## Time Management

### 3. Mary Callahan Erdoes uses the calendar for day-to-day management

"The biggest tool to manage time is calendar management. Focus on controlling your calendar. Create a list of you expect from others and what others expect from you. If you don't control your calendar, it will end up controlling you."

### 4. Barack Obama limits his outfits

Barack Obama is the former president of the united states.

"I pare down decisions by wearing only blue or gray suits. Since I have too many decisions to make, I prefer to exclude eating and wearing decisions out of it by paring down my decisions."

### 5. Jack Groetzinger tracks his time

Jack is the co-founder and CEO of SeatGeek.

"I have an estimated period for each of my tasks. I have software that records when I start and finish each item on my task list. I push myself to accomplish an efficiency goal for each day. My efficiency goal is actual minutes divided by expected minutes. I have fun gamifying my to-do list because I own all the spots on the leaderboard."

### 6. Gary Vaynerchuk uses other people's time

Gary Vaynerchuk is a business coach and the CEO of VaynerchukMedia.

"I scale my time efficiency using other people. I can focus on my personal and professional priorities by having others do the tasks that must be done. One of my assistants works full-time as my health coach. He oversees my exercise and nutrition. The other assistant follows me around and films me. As my time becomes more valuable, I may hire a full-time driver rather than waiting for a ride."

**Pro Tip:** If you can't afford to hire full-time assistants, you can hire virtual assistants or outsource some of your tasks to them.

### 7. Steve Ballmer creates a time budget

Steve is the ex-CEO of Microsoft. Steve has a spreadsheet accessible by his assistants where he budgets time to those who need to speak with him or meet him. Thus, he manages his time by spending most of his time on important things.

### 8. Adora Cheung is strict about meetings

Adora Cheung is the CEO of Homejoy, an online platform that connects customers with home service providers. Adora sends a Google Doc to potential meeting participants. These participants write down the agenda for the meeting. After prioritizing the topics, Adora does not discuss any plan that's not on the list.

### 9. Tony Hsieh uses Yesterbox

Tony Hsieh is the CEO of the famous shoe and clothing line, Zappos. Tony recommends responding to yesterday's emails today. Hence, today's emails won't clutter your focus for the day. He terms this technique as "Yesterbox." One capable app that can help you to achieve inbox zero is called boomerang. It helps you to give proper attention to specific emails by resending those emails into your inbox as new emails at your specified time.

### 10.   Arianna Huffington eats meals away from her desk

Arianna Huffington is the author of 15 books, the founder of the *Huffington Post* and the founder/CEO of Thrive Global. She recommends *not* working while taking meal breaks during the day. *"Take a colleague and have lunch at a table far away from your desk or go to a cafeteria. This shouldn't take more than 20 minutes. Doing this is more recharging than eating lunch while working,* which is what many of us do. It can be the difference between having a productive or an unproductive end to your day."

## 11. Mark Cuban uses email for most interactions

Mark Cuban is an American investor and businessman. He co-owns 2929 Entertainment, owns the Dallas Mavericks (an American basketball team), and is an investor in "Shark Tank." Rather than waste time in long meetings or on lengthy phone calls, Mark Cuban uses email for most conversations and become more productive. *"Email saves me hours every day. No phone calls, no meetings, and I set my schedule. Unless I'm picking up a check, all other things are email. I love it, and I live on it."*

## 12. Jeff Bezos uses the "Two Pizza Rule"

Jeff is the founder, CEO, and president of Amazon.com. He is also an investor and charity donor. Rather than waste his time in meetings, Bezos maximizes his time by not attending big meetings. To him, a meeting is big if two pizzas can't feed the participants at the meetings.

## 13. Nick Huzar capitalizes on Sundays

Nick is the CEO and co-founder of OfferUp, which connects local buyers and sellers. *"Plan your work and stick to the plan. I ensure that I create a quiet period for myself on Sundays. During this period, I examine each department at OfferUp to determine the team's priorities. Then, during the week, I support each team to implement these priorities. Also, I'm a sucker for routines. With routines, I'm able to eliminate excuses. For example, the first thing I always do each night is to pack for the next day's gym."*

# 10 Morning Routines of Groundbreaking Entrepreneurs

Starting your day right is the key to uber-productive days. Your actions at the start of the day will determine whether you will achieve extraordinary or mediocre results. Here's how ten highly successful entrepreneurs maximize their days right from the time they get out of bed.

### 1. Create a to-do list the previous night

"On alternating days, I work out for an hour and jog to the office. While at the office, I review my to-do list from the previous night. Thus, I can identify my most important tasks and finish them before anything else." - Barbara Corcoran, founder of the Corcoran Group.

### 2. Start your day with maximum energy

"By waking up early and playing basketball, my starts with the right energy and clarity. After showering, I eat a 3-egg breakfast, which fills me to satisfaction and sharpens my focus. Then, I proceed to achieve a zero-inbox. I help my team with any challenges they're facing. Thus, I have an idea of my challenges for the day. I ponder on my tasks' list for the day and face them squarely." - Tim Draper, founding partner of DFJ - a legendary VC firm.

### 3. Choose a routine that fits your personality type

"Your personality type can be emotional, social, action, or practical. If you are the emotional type, you are sensitive and might be introverted. Hence, your routine will involve lots of quiet time and introspection. If you are the social type, your daily routine will be people-based. For example, you will love working out in the gym in the presence of at least five people. If you are the action-type personality, you will love a morning routine of variety. You will love to start your day with a combination of jogging, jujitsu, or reading various books, especially books outside your industry. Practical-type people love a well-structured daily routine. The most important aspect of any routine is sticking with your plan. We all tend to have a morning routine until life happens. So, use your personality type to determine your most effective morning routine." - Tai Lopez, investor and advisor to many multimillion-dollar businesses with an eight-figure online empire.

## 4. Tune up your brain

"Since I know my day will be busy and probably, unpredictable, I start my day by going for a cold swim in the pool. Then, over a cup of coffee, I play the crossword puzzle in the Los Angeles Times; this rarely exceeds 20 minutes. Then, I get into my office to start working." - Mark Sisson. Mark Sisson is the publisher of marksdailyapple.com (a paleo blog), the best-selling author of the New Primal Blueprint and the founder of the Primal Blueprint.

## 5. Use nutrition to fire up your brain

"I drink one ounce of water which contains a cleansing mineral. I flush out my system by drinking a quart of structured purified water. Then, I wake up every muscle with a 45-pound kettlebell and 20 minutes of Turkish getups. I provide my brain with the ultimate brain nutrient by taking three milliliters of oceans alive marine phytoplankton. After my shower, I use 30 sprays of ease magnesium for my abdomen before taking a supplement to repair my cells. I eat two farm-fertilized organic chicken eggs and three different types of fruit for my breakfast. Lastly, I take a cup of green smoothie." - Ian Clark. Ian is the founder and CEO of Activation Products.

## 6. Jumpstart your metabolism

"After getting out of bed by 5:30 am, I drink 20 ounces of water to set my metabolism into action. I write my gratitude list for the morning. Then, I determine my two main priorities for the day. These priorities must move me in the direction of my goals before I *can call my day awesome."* - Jon Braddock, founder, and CEO of My Life & Wishes.

## 7. Verbalize your day's intention
*"I spend a few minutes to show gratitude for health and body before I get out of bed. Then, I speak out my intention for the day. While setting the intentions for my goals, I drink a glass of water, light some candles, and daydream. I check my emails for important messages before swinging into full work mode."* - Elle Russ, Coach and Best-Selling Author of the Paleo Thyroid Solution.

## 8. Start early
*"I get up at 4:15 am and spend 15 minutes of gratitude. By 5 am, I am at the gym to have a bodybuilding session with a personal trainer until 6 am. Between 6:30 and 7 am, I meditate and envision how to achieve my goals and dreams. I spend 30 minutes (7:15 am to 7:45 am) with my family before starting work by 8 am."* - Adele McLay, Author, Speaker, and Business Growth Consultant.

## 9. Start with meditation
*"After meditation, I use my five-minute journal before exercising and drinking a protein shake. Then, I help others in my way. Either by making an important introduction, sending a written note of gratitude or posting a #ploughshare online. I spend some time to write or draw images. Lastly, I take one major step to achieve my goal."* - Chris Plough, Serial Entrepreneur and Entrepreneur Advisor.

## 10. Block off times of solitude
*"Being a father of young children, an entrepreneur, and a doctor, my days can become highly disorder without proper planning. After getting up by 6:30 am, I spend a minimum of 30 minutes in complete and peaceful solitude before having a cup of coffee. To get into the right state of mind, I pray, read some educational materials, review*

*my goals for that day, and practice mindful meditation. I strongly engage in a positive-thinking mental state to foster immense power into my mind. When I am not on intermittent fasting, my breakfast is usually light and consists of a few nutritional supplements depending on my current blood test results. Then, I maximize the day by working with full zeal and energy."* - Dr. Nick Zurowski, founder of NuVision Health Center.

I encourage you to use any of these morning routines as they are or more importantly, modify them to suit your lifestyle so that you can enjoy more productive and creative mornings.

# Chapter 7 - Regaining Control of The Future

## 15 Effective Time Management Habits

If you have read this far, you would have identified some time management habits already. Some were discussed in the previous chapter as examples from business masters, successful people, and groundbreaking entrepreneurs. Others have been discussed in previous chapters. Hence, they won't be repeated in this chapter. Instead, you will discover more proven time management tips that you can incorporate into your daily life.

### 1. Learn to speed-read

While you cannot avoid all the barrage of information being thrown at you, you can sort them and go through them at your pace and time. Learning to speed-read is one of the most important skills you can develop. Have you ever taken a course in speed reading? If no, enroll for one now. With new technologies now available, you can read up to 1,000 words per minute and comprehend most of what you have read.

### 2. Stack your reading

Print and file important pieces of information, summaries, or valuable items. Alternatively, you can collate them in a separate file on your computer and read them later. Rather than lose focus on your current task, you can file away that piece of information and read them later. Once this becomes a habit, you will be amazed at how much you can give to what you read and how much more you read. Whether you are reading the paper version or electronic version of your newspapers, skim and read what's relevant to you. When you are reading the news, bear in mind that most of the information is always in the headline and first paragraph. Most times, you rarely need to read the remaining details to understand the story fully.

### 3. Only read what is important and relevant

The design of all magazines and newspapers is to make you read each page of the magazine or newspaper. The reason is for you to view all the advertisements in magazines or newspapers. Thus, you must read what matters to you only. After reviewing the table of contents, head to the information that is relevant to your life and work. The "rip and read" technique is an exceptional technique for printed materials. Rip out and file articles you intend to read. Then, carry the file with you to read during your timeouts. Similarly, read book reviews before spending time to read the complete book. You can get the main gist of the book by reading the book's review. Instead of scouring the web to read reviews, it is more convenient to subscribe to book review services.

### 4. Organize your work environment

For many people, they believe that a messy work environment and a cluttered desk aids their work efficiency. However, various research has shown that when people work in a clean, ordered environment and focus only on one task, their productivity almost triples instantly. People with a cluttered work environment spend copious time seeking the materials they need to work effectively. Psychologically, a cluttered work environment affirms your belief that you lack organization. Hence, you are continuously distracted by all the items you are seeing.

### 5. Maximize your mornings

Set your alarm clock for a couple of hours earlier than normal when you have deadlines to hit and projects to complete. I've found this to be more effective than trying to work extra in the evening when you're too tired to focus. You can get some dedicated time by going to bed an hour earlier than your usual time. In the early morning hours, your mind is alert, you're refreshed, the house is quiet, and you are at peak productivity. Spend this extra hour on one item of your task list. A half-hour earlier in the day is an additional 23 days over the year. This is as good as buying time. Imagine that!

## 6. Map out your weekly meals

Consider your schedules, special occasions, and items on the grocery list to plan your meal for the week. Remember to review the pantry to ensure that all the ingredients for items on your grocery list are completely available. Also, go to the supermarket with a proper plan, there should be no impulse purchase. When you make it a habit to plan your meal once a week, you won't waste time pondering on what to eat. A side benefit is that you eat healthier.

You can apply the weekly meal plan to other aspects of your life. For example, choose a day to plan the clothes you will wear for the week. Then, ensure you wash them and make them ready for your use.

## 7. Be in the present

Abandon all your baggage from the previous day in the past. Don't allow your previous day's failures, embarrassments, losses, disappointments, and mistakes to affect the joy you will likely experience today. Start your day by expecting to experience a day of relationship building, fulfillment, and success. Maximize your time to enjoy the best return on each day of your life.

## 8. Establish rules for your time

Establish rules for your time when creating your schedule. Turn off your cell phone during your timeout, for example, during breakfast. Set aside blocks of time that you will not be available to people and devices.

## 9. Audit your time

Assess your current time spending habits for the next seven days. Record your activities in a journal or on your phone. Split your activities into one-hour blocks. Then, answer the following questions:

- What did you accomplish?
- Was it a complete waste of time?
- Did you spend the time to your satisfaction?

Use the priority matrix discussed in chapter four to log your activities in the appropriate quadrant. Add the numbers after seven days. So, which quadrant did you spend the most time? Don't be surprised by your answer.

## 10. Eliminate your bad habits

Bad habits are one of our biggest time wasters. Those bad habits eliminate our precious little time. Hence, if you are serious about achieving big goals in your life, and spend your time wisely, ensure you eliminate those bad habits. Examples of time-wasting habits include going out to drink with friends frequently, playing games, excessively surfing social media, and Netflix binge-watching.

## 11. Find a mentor

When you don't have someone to guide you, you can quickly get distracted and dissuaded. But it's easier to stay on track with your time when you can personally rely on someone who's been through the same process. Thus, he can help you achieve your goals faster.

## 12. Don't wait for inspiration

You are wasting time by waiting to start a project. Since there is no perfect time to do anything, throw away the excuses that are preventing you from getting started. While I'm not suggesting that you should be impatient, you should identify what you intend to accomplish and take immediate action towards it.

### 13. Engage in hobbies

Hobbies engage in parts of your brain that you don't use for work. Thus, you become more creative and can solve problems with ease. You can achieve success by spending some time outside of your comfort zone. If you're a software developer, go out and socialize. If you're pianist, practice martial arts. If you're a lawyer, learn to dance.

### 14. Have a great time

Don't become obsessed about marking off all the tasks on your task list. Balance your work and life to enjoy your day. It's not worth it to complete an oversized workload one day only to have an unproductive, burnt-out day the next day. Work at your best pace. When you rush through tasks, you become stressed and produce substandard work.

### 15. Meditate

A few minutes of meditation can improve your focus and calmness. Thus, your work becomes more efficient, and your contribution is more significant. Also, meditation brings your mind back to the present to help you avoid several distractions. When your mind is in the present, you can accomplish a lot more within a small time-span. Meditation improves your awareness. Thus, we rarely make mistakes at work, and you save the time you're supposed to use to correct your errors. Meditation can also strengthen your intuition. A strong intuition enhances your decision-making ability and consequently, saves you time.

# Defeating Perfectionism Once and for All

Though our current world expects us to be perfect in always, it doesn't mean that perfectionism is the way to a successful life. Like an obsessive-compulsive disorder, your desire for perfection can mess you up. And since it makes you lose perspective as you get deeper into it, it messes up those around you. Since none of us can become perfect, you will only be driving yourself crazy, trying to achieve an elusive goal. Perfectionism can lead to depression. Research by Sydney Blatt, a psychologist at Yale University showed that perfectionists are more likely to kill themselves than regular people.

To avoid the perfectionist trap, implement these seven proven steps:

## 1. Practice failing

Doing exercises where you will likely fail is one of the most effective ways to defeat perfectionism. So, learn a new skill that requires a lot of falling and embarrassment. It will teach you that tolerance of failure, self-compassion, and patience are part of the learning curve.

For example, I joined a racing group of paddlers despite having been on a paddleboard only a couple of times. This group consists of people who paddle at least 21 miles in the ocean and perform those cool 360 turns on their boards. I spent most of the evening in the water and not on it, but I am now more comfortable with failing. I realize that the world won't end because I am the worst person in a group of athletes. I will do my best to translate this lesson into other areas of my life, where I am anxious or depressed due to perfectionism.

## 2. Differentiate between goals and dreams

Since it is highly probable that they won't happen, grand ideas usually create lots of angst. For example, one of my friends used to dream of playing professional basketball. Nothing wrong in having a dream, right? But he started having behavioral issues because he was placed in the C team of his basketball team. When he's on his good behavior, he will practice his shots and improve his techniques for hours daily. But he always plays badly during games because he was exerting too much pressure on himself. When I feel like my expectations were weighing too much on me, I usually write down my goals on a piece of paper. Then, I will check off the realistic ones. But I will tweak the silly ones to avoid putting myself under undue pressure.

### 3. Be a hard worker

It is often said that smart people cut corners. However, knowing which corners to cut is the art of being a star performer. Hence, the way out is to analyze your goal in all honesty critically. Then, identify any perfectionism in the plan for each purpose. Most times, we hide under perfectionism to avoid taking actions to accomplish our real goals. The truth is, a proper plan, hard work, and a bit of luck are required to achieve any real intent. But most perfectionists don't agree that luck is involved in achieving any goal.

### 4. Keep yourself in check

Keep yourself in check when your self-doubt is becoming more real, or you start having reasons to believe your inner critic. Use these questions to give yourself a reality check:

- Are my thoughts based on facts, or are they the figment of my imagination?
- Why am I making unfavorable verdicts?
- Is the situation as bad as I imagine it?
- What's the worst thing that can happen? Is it likely to happen?
- Will this be important in the next five years? Will this be an issue at vital moments of my life? Examples of essential moments include childbirth, moving to another city, or moving abroad.

By the time I complete answering these questions, I often realize that I was only trying to validate various falsehoods in my head. Sometimes, I even forgot how I got into this frightening state in the first place. Apart from giving reassuring our self-esteem, this reality test also makes less dependent on others for affirmative compliments.

## 5. Be kind to yourself

As a perfectionist, you often criticize others. It is a proven fact that this criticism is a defense mechanism. It causes you to pick on the shortcomings in others rather than accept those shortcomings in yourself or accept that no human being is perfect. The more you identify your weaknesses, the more you look out for it in those around you. You do this because you have created an ideal image of the perfect person and life, but you can't seem to separate this idealized version from reality. A simple and effective way to reduce this habit significantly is to be kind to yourself. When you like your "flawed and imperfect" self, you're much less likely to be the irritable person who critically analyzes others.

So, try saying one thing you love about yourself each morning. It can be something about your face or a poem about yourself. Anytime you feel you need a boost during the day, repeat this affirmation. Note that nothing stops you from using the same declaration every day or having seven daily affirmations. Thus, you only repeat one affirmation every seven days. Rather than living an unforgiving, locked-down, and hard-hearted life, start being kind to yourself.

## 6. Refuse fear

Are you afraid of:

- Choosing a partner,
- Making the wrong life decision or
- Starting a new project?

If yes, then, you are exhibiting some of a perfectionist's trait. All the factors above have a common theme: a fear of failure. Thus, we rely on others to guide us and make our decisions for us. But refusing to allow fear to dictate your moves or choice is one of the best ways to combat such behavior.

One way to develop the habit of preventing fear to lead is to automate the start of the sequence. For example, a basketball player is ready to rise and shoot just as he has done a hundred times a day during practice by coming to the free-throw line, touching his socks, shorts, receiving the ball and bouncing it exactly three times.

Similarly, a pro golfer may be chatting with the scorekeeper, a friendly official, his playing partner or his caddie while walking along the fairway. But the moment he stands behind the ball and takes a deep breath, he's telling himself just one thing: focus.

In each of these examples, the athletes were able to replace doubt and fear with comfort and routine. They could do this because they've learned how to automate the start of their sequence. Rather than pretend not to be in the mood because I am afraid to start, I start with the smallest step towards the goal.

### 7. Be proud of your accomplishments

When we were young, we sketched what we intend to become in the future. However,, most of us never become what we've sketched out. Rather than being an astronaut or petrochemical engineer, you are probably a barista who barely spends time with his loved ones because you work for long periods. As a perfectionist, you need to accept that fact. Stop comparing yourself with others thinking you haven't achieved enough or you may never achieve anything. Instead, be comfortable in your skin and be proud of your accomplishments.

Create a list of your accomplishments in the past week, month, or year. Even the simple things count. The book you finished, that small project you completed with your team or maintaining a clean home. These are your accomplishments without being the neuro-surgeon you imagined when you were five years old.

Like any change, trust and self-examination are some of the requirements to tame any perfectionist tendencies. But if you meet challenges on the way and it seems you aren't moving forward, don't beat yourself up or take yourself too seriously. Find the means to succeed and enjoy the process. Keep in mind that you are solely responsible for your success or failure. So, don't give up.

# Tools and Techniques to Take Back Time for Good

Ever heard any or all of these phrases before:

- The emails flooding my inbox is making me lose focus.
- Let me check my social media feed. It won't take 5 minutes!

If you have heard any of these phrases, then, you know the person lacks proper time management. Time management involves organizing tasks and allocating time to specific activities (professional or personal).

Before delving into those tools and techniques, remember that tasks, time, people, and information are the four key areas to any successful time management system. Hence, you should have any of these four essential tools:

- **Notebook**

A good notebook is the most frequently missing too in people's time management systems. Yes, it is good to have a bunch of post-its or a pad of paper on your desk. But you should keep all your notes in one place. Thus, when you need to retrieve any piece of information, you can go to this place.

- **Address Book**

Most people do not see the value of a good address book because we now live in a uber-connected world. However, when you need to connect with valuable contact, LinkedIn, Instagram, Facebook, or Twitter may disappoint you. Your best option is to save all contact's phone numbers and email addresses in a safe place and treat them like gold.

- **Calendar**

If you don't know how and where you spend your time, it would be difficult to manage it. It is easier for you to schedule, plan, and track your time with a good calendar. You cannot only track the time for your meetings, but you can also track the time for your tasks and projects.

- **To-do list**

A good to-do list is a cornerstone of any productivity system. This one-time management tool should complete your arsenal of tools. However, don't forget to reread the common reasons why to-do lists fail in Chapter 3 of this book.

Thus, you can avoid making those mistakes with your to-do list. Lastly, your to-do list should be with you all the time. Double-check your time management toolkit to ensure that you have all these four essential time management tools.

When you can plan and accomplish your daily routines within specified time frames, then, you are a good manager of time. Thus, you can carry out your activities with more significant commitment. Fortunately, technology has made it possible to optimize every minute of the day. In this section, you will discover seven tools and techniques that I use, and I am convinced will improve your time management skills and productivity.

## 1. A time management system

A proper organization of your daily tasks is one of the steps you can take to improve your productivity and not suck at time management. In any self-organization process, creating to-do lists is an essential step. You might have to try a few to-do list methods to discover the one that's most suitable for you. Your to-do list could be a fancy electronic version on your mobile device or computer. But it could be done using old-fashioned pen and paper which you check off after completing each task.

An overview of each significant activity is your first step when you have high-level projects. Then, you can split them into specific tasks and arrange them in the order in which they have to be performed. Don't forget to add deadlines to each task.

Here are three examples of such systems that you can use

- **The Now Habit by Neil Fiore.** This system teaches you to use a reverse order to build your to-do list. Fill your calendar with realistic leisure time, committed activities, and scheduled chores. Then, use different lifestyle and scheduling rules to assign your tasks into the remaining times.
- **The Final Version by Mark Forster.** From the task list, you have written for the day, go through it, and identify the most crucial task. Complete that task, then, identify the next most important task. Complete it and repeat the process till you complete all the task for that day.
- **Getting Things Done by David Allen.** Perform a brain dump of your tasks on paper. Then, rearrange them in order of importance. Next, set a deadline for completion and get to work. Review your execution plans periodically and where necessary, make adjustments.

## 2. Wunderlist

With Wunderlist, you can create task lists, organize them into folders, and set up reminders to alert you when the deadline is close. Wunderlist has an enchanting user interface, and all its features work effectively on all devices (cell phone, tablet, or computer).

## 3. Remember The Milk

The free plan allows you to create tasks and synchronize them on any platform, including your emails. Thus, you can access your tasks anytime. Perfect for managing personal tasks, Remember The Milk is available for Android and iOS.

## 4. RescueTime

Do you always feel that time passes very quickly, and it's almost impossible for you to complete your daily activities? Then, the RescueTime app is your best option. With it, you can track your tasks online. It gauges your progress and reveals the time you spend procrastinating.

## 5. Todoist or Trello

Todoist is both a cloud-based app and a mobile app. You can access your Todoist tasks on multiple operating systems and even share your tasks with other colleagues. Also, it displays delivery times. You can easily play around with the features because it has an intuitive layout. First, type in your project, then, split them into specific tasks and attach a deadline to each of them. Now, assign a level of priority to each task (there are four priority levels there). You can move the tasks around to suit your available time.

If you have a small team, you can use Trello to visualize your team's projects. Within Trello, you can assign tasks to each team member, set up boards that represent projects and set up various lists within each board. There are a series of cards for each list. The cards represent tasks. For example, you can create a board for a specific project, split the board into lists (the stages of the project), then, arrange each individual's tasks on a series of cards.

## 6. Relaxation breaks

You must take time out of your work; it will increase your productivity. After a period of sustained concentration, your body needs a release, and your mind needs a timeout. Sometimes, you develop fresh ideas from your timeout. The best way to help this process is to take a 5-minute walk away from your workspace. If you don't take breaks intentionally, your mind will do so for you by wandering when you are tired.

Use the FocusMe app to set enforced breaks or break reminders.

## 7. Process management technique

When you have personal tasks or business tasks, then, the time management tools and techniques discussed above are excellent. However, when your business grows, and you need to manage bulk processes or team time, then, the process management technique is a more effective system. This technique maps out the primary operations of a company and set deadlines for each task. Also, it adds an alert configuration to serve as the basis of prioritization. Here's how the alert configuration works for an airfare booking task:

- The person in charge receives an email when you reach 50% of the task deadline
- You will see a red visual indicator when you reach 70% of the task deadline
- At 80% of the task deadline, the person in charge receives a new message.

## 8. Evernote

This free productivity tool allows you to organize your images, thoughts, and ideas in various formats (audio, text, or pictures). Also, you can record your speeches, interviews, and meetings. You can even share your voice or text attachments with your friends. Optimize your time by syncing the Remember The Milk app with Evernote. Arguably, one of Evernote's most useful and popular features is its web clipper. This is similar to bookmarks in web browsers. Web clipper allows you to "clip" paragraphs of text, images or entire webpages to Evernote. Clipped items can be organized, stored, and searched like regular notes. You can even add annotations to "clipped" items in Evernote. You can integrate Evernote with Gmail, Outlook, Google Drive, Microsoft teams, Salesforce, Slack, and most other apps on your mobile devices or PC.

## 9. MyLifeOrganized (MLO)

If you struggle to organize your goals, work with your to-do lists, or manage all your tasks, this app is your best option. This productivity tool helps you to focus on the actual steps to accomplish your goals. It considers your set priorities (urgency, importance, start date, and terms of completion) to identify your first task automatically.

# **Conclusion**

You can become a master time manager when you practice the techniques and use the tools recommended in this book. Reclaim your time from busywork, have more hours to spend with your loved ones and improve your personal life. The main reason for having improved time management skills is to increase our experience of pleasure, happiness, and the overall quality of our lives. Three things largely determine the quality of your life:

- Inner life
- Health
- Relationships


- **Inner life** involves feeling good about your personality and character, liking yourself and getting along with yourself. It takes time and reflection to improve your inner life.
- **Health.** No level of success is worth having poor health. Most times, the best use of your time involves going to bed early and having a good night's sleep. Also, take time out to get proper rest, exercise regularly, and eat the right foods.
- **Relationships.** Make out time for your loved ones. The most influential people in your life are those you care about and those who care about you. So, don't get caught up in so much at the expense of vital relationships with your loved ones. A balanced life is a great life. You will find greater fulfillment, satisfaction, and joy by enhancing the quality of your life. Let me leave you with the words of a wise old doctor. "Having spoken to lots of people when they are about to die, no businesses man on his deathbed ever wished to spend more time in his office."

You just learned proven steps and strategies for managing your time efficiently and effectively. That means you can now improve your productivity and achieve your goals. Still, packing away all this information in your head won't do you any good if you don't put it to use. Hence, I encourage you to return to chapter 1 and identify the reasons why you're failing at time management. Then, review the steps in subsequent chapters and start implementing them right away.

When you implement the steps and strategies in this book, you will see a marked improvement in your life. You feel more in control and have more time for yourself. Start every day with an accomplishment that gives you energy. This can be a physical workout or meditation.

At first, implementing these techniques can make you feel uncomfortable. But the rewards can make your day highly productive. You will experience greater confidence because you are more energetic. Once your weekly plans and activities become a habit, challenge yourself to create a monthly plan.

Over time, you should develop a 3-month, 6-month, and an annual plan. Take a weekend off at the end of the year to reflect on the previous year and plan for the new one. Ensure you schedule your events, vacations, and projects into your yearly plan. Planning your future with a well-designed plan can calm your nerves in this world of uncertainty.

When you are in charge of your time, you have improved confidence that's noticeable to others. Saving time involves investing some time to plan, make changes, and improve your life. The most significant single piece of advice I can give you at this point is: do not get lost in the weeds! By this, I mean, do not get lost in every tiny detail.

## Time Management

Getting good at managing your time requires you to take action rather than trying to get every last detail in order. Even if you are feeling unsure about whether or not you're doing things correctly, it is far more important to get started. I can't stress this enough. I promise that results will come with just some practice and some experience. That is the only thing separating you from achieving the goals you desire. Don't worry about whether or not everything is 100% perfect or feeling skeptical whether or not this will work for you. Just do it. All of these excuses will only stunt your growth. Take action now — not tomorrow. Your success depends on the action you take today.

I'm going to challenge you to be accountable. Call a trusted friend and share your goal of better time management. That's right; you're going to be held accountable. Because this time you won't fail. This time you're going to get better at managing your time finally. No matter who you are, you can manage your time with greater efficiency. You deserve this. So, go ahead and get started now, because higher productivity and a better life is waiting for you!